FREE MARKETS, FREE MEN
Frederic Bastiat, 1801–1850

by

George Roche

The Hillsdale College Press
The Foundation for Economic Education

Published by the Hillsdale College Press and the Foundation for Economic Education.

Library of Congress Catalog Card Number 93-078834
ISBN 0-916308-73-1

Cover design by Somberg Design
Printed by McNaughton & Gunn, Inc.

*To Leonard Read, who years ago rescued an obscure
Frenchman from the historical ash-heap and who was among
the first to realize his enormous importance.*

Contents

Foreword

As schoolchildren, we learned about the courageous and idealistic Marquis de Lafayette, who came to the aid of the colonies during the American Revolution. We also learned about Napoleon, whose dread ambition was to rule an empire founded on the power of the state and Madame Guillotine. Later, in high school or college, some of us also read the works of the likes of Montesquieu and Tocqueville. But very few of us know anything at all about Frederic Bastiat, a 19th-century Frenchman whose ideas were destined to play a decisive role in the history of the West.

Bastiat was one of the first of a new breed of intellectuals—an economist. He devoted his attention to one of the most fascinating of all subjects: how people make decisions in the marketplace, and how their individual decisions combine to constitute a national economy. He knew that economics is above all about the power of individuals. Although each person has limited knowledge, he has only to do a good job at his specific task to partake in the benefits of others' knowledge and success. He doesn't have to ask the state, "What must I do to prosper?" He decides for himself. Sometimes he fails, of course, but it is an old truth that without failure there can be no success.

Among Bastiat's most important observations was that when "do-everything" government assumes control over things that are properly *our* responsibility, we lose faith in our capacity to make our own decisions. A century and a half ago he warned, "I have seen countries in which the people think that agriculture can make no progress unless the government supports experimental farms; that there will soon be no horses if the government does not provide the studs; that fathers will not have their children educated or will have them taught only immorality, if the government does not decide what is proper to learn." Would that he could warn our Congress and the present administration about the dangers of trying to make peoples' decisions for them!

It's high time for all of us to pay attention to Frederic Bastiat. He addressed taxation, trade, welfare, labor, education, the rise of bureaucracy—precisely the issues public policy analysts, from ethicists to economists, are writing about today—and, for my money, he wrote much more presciently and wisely about them. This forgotten Frenchman, as Hillsdale College President George Roche makes clear, is full of truths that are not merely relevant but are absolutely vital to our future.

September, 1993   Dick Armey
                                 U.S. House of Representatives

Introduction

A little over twenty years ago, this book was first published under the title, *Frederic Bastiat: A Man Alone.* You may rightly wonder why it has seen the light of day once more.

The first reason is simple. I receive literally hundreds of calls and letters each year from people who are interested in the study of the free market, especially in its historic origins. They have usually heard of the Scottish moral philosopher Adam Smith who published his famous treatise, *Wealth of Nations,* in 1776, but beyond that, they know little about the other key 18th- and 19th-century thinkers who were forging their way into the new and uncharted intellectual territory of economics.

Frederic Bastiat was one of the most intrepid explorers. The son of a respectable but undistinguished family, Bastiat spent his first 45 years in quiet preparation for an enormous flash of productive activity that occurred during his last five years. He wrote about economics and political theory as a keen observer of the human condition rather than as a abstract theorist or an impassioned ideologue. Clearly he saw that the problem with theorists and ideologues is not that they are always wanting to change the nature of things, but that they are always wanting to change the nature of man. He summed up their arrogance:

> For although mankind, in itself incompetent, has been on the wrong track for six millennia, a prophet has come who has shown

men the way to salvation; and if the flock will only be docile enough to follow the shepherd, he will lead it into the promised land where prosperity may be attained without effort, and where order, security, and harmony are the easy reward of improvidence.

This view, he warned, inspires the dangerous notion that "all men have to do is to permit the reformers to change, as Rousseau said, *their physical and moral constitution.*"

*   *   *

The second reason for reissuing this book is that Bastiat had a great deal to say that is relevant to the times in which we live. The themes he wrote about—the gradual but steady growth of government, the debate over free trade and protectionism, the rebuilding of societies that have suffered socialist-style revolutions—these are issues that we also face, and his liberal perceptions about them are as fresh and insightful as if he had just penned them.

"Liberal" in the late 20th century implies a readiness to use government as a problem-solving device and as a handy and absolutely necessary tool to save the citizens of the republic from the "dangerous" effects of the free market. In the 19th century, "liberal" had a precisely opposite meaning. For Bastiat, the encroachment of the state in the lives of its citizens was not a solution to society's problems, but instead was the problem itself. (Thus he anticipated Ronald Reagan's famous dictum, "Government is not the solution . . . " by nearly 150 years.)

Though the meaning of the word "liberal" has changed, the underlying argument has not. We are still trying to decide whether or not government should be the final arbiter of men's affairs. It is the central argument of our time, just as it was in Bastiat's day. Typically, he addressed it in a fashion as down-to-earth as our daily lives. Always quick to defend the consumer, the forgotten man of most modern economic analyses, he wrote in terms at once understandable and entertaining. One essay on the perils of protectionism published in the 1840s is still quoted today. Called "The Petition of the Candlemakers," the complaint was that they were "suffering from the ruinous competition of a foreign rival" who could produce light so cheaply and under such superior, i.e., unfair conditions that he was "flooding the domestic market," probably with the connivance of France's political and commercial enemy, England. The rival? It was, of course, the sun.

Bastiat often turned a withering blast of ridicule on those who presumed to know what was best for everyone else. To be laughed at is the one thing which big government has never been able to stand. Writing in a more serious vein, long before government reached its current enormous proportions, Bastiat predicted:

> The state quickly understands the use it can make of the role the public entrusts to it. It will be the arbiter, the master of all destinies. It will take a great deal; hence a great deal will remain for itself. It will multiply the number of its agents; it will enlarge the scope of its prerogatives; it will end by acquiring overwhelming proportions.

He would be disheartened, but not surprised, to learn that we in the United States spend 40 percent of our GNP to maintain federal, state and local government, that the cost of government regulation to consumers is $400 billion annually, and that the federal debt is approximately four trillion dollars.

*   *   *

Though few of today's readers will even recognize the name of Frederic Bastiat, he was one of those men fated to stand at the crossroads of sweeping historical events and radically conflicting ideologies. Between 1801 and 1850, he lived through three major revolutions and their inevitable traveling companions, anarchy and dictatorship. As a politician, he watched citizens take to the barricades again and again. As an economist, he realized that the changes induced by the Industrial Revolution were making a totally new society in Europe. There could be no road back to the past, no staying the hand of change.

He saw before most of his contemporaries that Western men had their destinies in their own hands as never before. Prosperity or disaster awaited the new industrial world, depending upon a single issue: would men allow the system to work, or would they, in Bastiat's phrase, "fear liberty" too much to give themselves this new beginning? This forgotten defender of free markets and free men would fully understand and appreciate our hopes and our fears today when, once again, the rise and fall of ideologies and nations has left the world poised on the edge of an uncertain yet potentially exciting future.

CHAPTER 1

A Time of Preparation

IN THE SOUTH OF FRANCE THE ROLLING GREEN hills are carefully kept by a frugal people. As those hills roll to the extreme southwestern tip of French soil, the gentle pastoral nature of the countryside is suddenly interrupted by the grim outline of the Pyrénées. Beneath the shadow of the mountains, on the shore of the Bay of Biscay, Claude Frederic Bastiat was born in 1801, on a warm June day in the small provincial town of Bayonne. Pierre Bastiat, Frederic's father, was a prominent merchant in the community.

The boy's mother died in 1808. The merchant then left Bayonne to move northward to an even smaller provincial town, Mugron. Perhaps he made the move inland in quest of drier air, since he suffered from a weak chest and had not been able to gain lasting physical strength, despite visits to a number of health resorts. Soon after his mother's death, the seven-year-old boy traveled to his new home with his ailing father. The town of Mugron was located in the valley of the Adour River, where the Bastiat estate had previously belonged to the Marquis of Poyanne. The Bastiat family had acquired the property after the Revolution. The estate was small, but well kept, and the little family soon settled into a new routine of quiet country living. Pierre Bastiat died in 1810, leaving young Frederic orphaned. The boy was taken in by his paternal grandfather and his maiden aunt. He attended several schools, before enrolling in the Benedictine college of Sorèze. It was

5

here that he developed such a great taste for reading and that he acquired the knowledge of English which was to play so large a role in forming his close ties with the English and American concepts of free trade and freedom in transactions.

It was also here that Bastiat found a close friend in M.V. Calmètes, who upon completing his studies went on to be a lawyer. But Bastiat did not stay at school long enough to graduate. At 17, he left Sorèze and went to work for his uncle in Bayonne, in the same firm where his father had previously been a partner.

Bayonne

It soon became apparent that young Bastiat was not well suited to a career as a merchant. His habits of quiet study and wide-ranging reading stayed with him in the business world, and he seemed more at home with literature than with ledgers. Nonetheless, affairs at his uncle's counting house sometimes attracted Frederic's attention. The Napoleonic Wars had ravaged French ports like Bayonne for two decades; controls of all sorts had set back Bayonne's commerce to a point well below its 18th-century levels. Even after 1815, controls of the French government were proving nearly as restrictive as the English blockade had ever been. For young Frederic, this first hand experience was convincing proof that the economic affairs of citizens always suffered when they became objects of public policy.

Observation of the hard times which had fallen upon Bayonne first turned Bastiat to serious study of political economy, especially the works of Jean-Baptiste Say and Adam Smith. Many of the ideas of a free economic order had been foreshadowed in the 18th-century work of the Physiocrats, especially

François Quesnay. In fact, Adam Smith had known Quesnay and acknowledged a substantial debt to him when *Wealth of Nations* was published in 1776. Smith in turn had greatly influenced Say, whose book *Traité d économie politique* proved so exciting and provocative for the young Bastiat. Bastiat devoured all the ideas on freedom which had been developing in France, England, and America for the past century.

Mugron

By 1824, Bastiat dreamed of going to Paris to pursue formal studies, but his grandfather, who was old and ill, asked him to return to Mugron. Thus, in his 23rd year, Bastiat found himself in the serene countryside of the Bastiat family estate, a retreat where he was destined to spend the next 20 years of his life in quiet study. Perhaps influenced by the Physiocrats, who had been steeped in agrarian attitudes, Bastiat at once undertook to revolutionize farming practices not only on his own estate, but through the entire area of the Adour River Valley. He also attempted to establish a local learned society on the Physiocratic model, specializing in both agricultural and economic studies. But his provincial neighbors soon discouraged the young man on both counts, who was heard to comment, "What would you have if you had a philharmonic society composed of the deaf?"

Soon after he returned to Mugron, he acquired another lifelong friend, Félix Coudroy, a brilliant young intellectual who lived on a neighboring estate. Coudroy was a recent graduate of the law school in Toulouse. A devotee of Rousseau, he was frankly socialistic and authoritarian. To Coudroy, any discussion of freedom and individuality implied anarchy and the collapse of the social order. To the liberal young Bastiat, deeply versed in Adam Smith and J. B. Say, Coudroy was a challenging specimen of everything wrong with 19th-century French thought. Again and again the two young friends met to argue the place of self-interest, the role of a free market, the necessity for individual dignity. In the end, Bastiat converted Coudroy to the liberal view, and in the process refined and strengthened his own understanding. For years they collaborated in their wide-ranging study of economics, philosophy, literature and politics.

But Bastiat could not have suspected that this lifetime of work was being stored against a day, when in the face of terrible pressures and illness, this slender, shy Frenchman would pour forth an enormous amount of published work at a critical moment in French history.

CHAPTER 2

Revolution: 1830

I waited for the blood, but the only thing that poured out was wine. This evening we fraternized with the officers of the garrison. Punch, wine, liquors, and especially the songs of Béranger added zest to the party.

THE FRENCH REVOLUTION, WHICH HAD BEGUN IN 1789 as an experiment in "popular" rule, brought a decade of unparalleled chaos and suffering to the people of France. The nation was "saved" from its sad fate by the inevitable dictator. In 1799, the dictator's name was Napoleon Bonaparte. The years of Bastiat's childhood were marked by military adventurism and authoritarian rule. The chaos of the revolution, followed by the endless wars of the Napoleonic regime, offered little real difference to the French people.

By 1815, the average Frenchman probably wondered what purpose the past 25 years of suffering had served. After all, the Revolution had begun with the effort to rid France of Bourbon rule. Thus the appointment between Madam Guillotine and Louis XVI. Yet, after the Treaty of Paris ended the Napoleonic era, the French found themselves with another Bourbon on the throne. The Restoration had placed Louis XVIII, brother of the beheaded French king, in his "rightful" position as ruler of France.

Louis XVIII also brought a return to many of the pre-revolutionary aristocratic privileges of property and class. The clergy promptly reinstated its authority over the 70 percent of the French population which composed the peasantry. The French peasant had never understood what was happening in Paris, and had tended to accept the turmoil and hardship of revolution and dictatorship as events on a par with bad weather: completely beyond control or comprehension, and therefore to be borne with a shrug. To such men, it must have seemed that Revolution had indeed brought more hardship than change to France.

It has been said of the Bourbons that they had learned nothing and had forgotten nothing, implying that the monarchy after 1815 had ignored everything which had occurred for the past 25 years. Yet there were changes. A large part of the revolutionary land settlements (including the land comprising the Bastiat estate) were retained in force. It is also true that, while the king retained executive authority, the new constitution limited royal power by calling for a two-house legislature with full authority to make the laws. In practice, however, the life of the typical Frenchman was little changed—a constant round of exertions to keep ahead of the tax collector. Whether the taxes were collected in the name of the people or the king made little practical difference.

Louis XVIII died in 1824, the year that young Frederic Bastiat returned to his estate in Mugron. But if Bastiat or any other Frenchman expected greater freedom after the old man's passing, he was sorely mistaken. Charles X, yet another brother of Louis XVI, mounted the throne and began an even more enthusiastically repressive regime.

Charles X began talking publicly of "the divine right of kings." He proposed that all nobles should be indemnified at state expense for property lost in the Revolution. He demanded that all books and newspapers sold in France must first gain the approval of a committee appointed by the king. In short, he did everything possible to antagonize the citizenry. Poor, tired France, willing to accept almost any indignity and interference in order to procure a few years of stability. But Charles X was too much even for revolution-weary Frenchmen.

In the legislative elections of 1830, Charles was completely repudiated. A wiser man might have heeded the warning; but not Charles X. On the morning of July 26, he attempted a coup d'état, dissolving the new legislature and abolishing all freedom to discuss the royal authority. The French, who by this time had developed a certain skill and confidence in revolutionary technique, rose up in the famous July days—27, 28, and 29—and made it clear that the royal services of Charles X were no longer required. In the *Devil's Dictionary,* Ambrose Bierce defines abdication as: "An act whereby a sovereign attests his sense of the high temperature of the throne." Charles X so attested at the end of July 1830, departing for England.

The *bourgeoisie* all over France celebrated his departure. Bastiat had listened with increasing uneasiness for the past two years as the petty nobility in the vicinity of Mugron had approvingly discussed a return to absolutism and the benefits likely to accrue to them as the result. As Bastiat neared the age of 30, he became increasingly convinced that some form of constitutional government, based upon solid bourgeois foundations, was absolutely necessary for France. Members of the French middle class, largely excluded from suffrage in the Restoration period, were ready to sing the praises of "democracy," since the word to them meant the transfer of power from the nobility to the bourgeoisie.

Not all those who opposed Charles X and his policies were so assured that the bourgeois rule would answer all problems.

A young man of Bastiat's generation, Alexis de Tocqueville, had also studied the course of events since 1789. He saw the whole era as a struggle to the death between France's nobility and her middle class. In his view, the nobility was attempting to retain control of French life in a futile effort to resist the rising power of the *bourgeoisie*. Tocqueville was to be proven quite right. Later, in his *Recollections,* he could write:

> In 1830 the triumph of the middle class had been definite and so thorough that all political power, every franchise, every prerogative, and the whole government was confined and, as it were, heaped up within the narrow limits of this one class, to the statutory exclusion of all beneath them and the actual exclusion of all above. Not only did it thus rule society, but it may be said to have formed it. It entrenched itself in every vacant place, prodigiously augmented the number of places and accustomed itself to live almost as much upon the Treasury as upon its own industry.

The middle class had long complained of the abuses of political power perpetrated by the French nobility. Now the middle class had taken political power unto itself. It remained to be proven that political power was safer in the hands of its new owners.

A Peaceful Revolutionary and a Citizen King

The excitement of the July Days in Paris quickly penetrated the provinces. Bastiat journeyed to Bayonne to join the revolutionary forces. The city of Bayonne had proclaimed itself in support of a change in government, and only the citadel of the city continued to fly the flag of the Bourbons. Rumors were also flying: perhaps Spanish troops were massing a few miles away at the frontier; perhaps the troops in the citadel were preparing to take over the city.

Bastiat and his friends prepared a proclamation and formed an association of some 600, who promptly declared themselves willing to take the government citadel by force if necessary. Instead, the citadel opened its gates. The officers of the garrison invited the young revolutionaries in to join a celebration. As Bastiat described it: "I waited for the blood, but the only thing that poured out was wine. This evening we fraternized with the officers of the garrison. Punch, wine, liquors, and especially the songs of Béranger added zest to the party." Afterwards, Bastiat, returned to Mugron and his peaceful studies.

The Revolution of 1830 was largely the work of the Parisian middle class. The *bourgeoisie* did not wish too radical a departure in French political life, preferring that the idea of a king be retained and asking only that the king be properly responsive to middle-class interests. How to achieve this delicate Gallic balance between change and continuity? The solution of this problem was the work of an old French hero, Lafayette. Now an old man, but still possessing enormous prestige with the French people, he was made head of the National Guard during the July Days. For a time, Lafayette might have imposed any government he chose.

Some Frenchmen desired a republic; others, like the wily Guizot and Thiers, favored middle-class power masked by monarchy. Acceding to their advice, Lafayette threw his support to Louis Philippe. Cousin of the Bourbons, a member of the Orléans family, Louis' credentials as royalty were in good order. Equally important, Louis Philippe was willing to view himself as the "Citizen King" and to serve as representative of the wealthier *bourgeoisie*. The new sovereign discarded royal robes, underplayed all pomp and ceremony, and posed as monarch by will of the people.

Like most of his contemporaries, Bastiat was solidly in favor of the new middle-class regime. He considered that France's troubles had originated in the prohibitive old regime of the Bourbons and looked to a reign of economic and political liberty under the wise government of the *bourgeoisie*. Parliamentary monarchy was all to the good now that the elite of the French nation, the enlightened *bourgeoisie*, occupied the seats of power. With the pear-shaped figure of Louis Philippe to symbolize the new order of prosperity and stability, middle class France settled back with a sigh of satisfaction. Though the current of revolution had begun in France, its reverberations were more lasting among some of its neighbors, notably Belgium, Italy and Germany. But for the French, the Revolution of 1830 was over almost as quickly as it had begun.

Louis Philippe and his queen were *bourgeois* in the extreme—no royal pomp and display for them. Unfortunately, the same fickle Parisians who had cheered for an end to all aristocracy were equally willing to jeer at the court of Louis Philippe, which they described as "ridiculous gatherings of tailors, drapers, and bootmakers." The new king's speaking style won as little respect as his court. One Paris wit described Louis Philippe's remarks before the Chamber of Deputies as "a sentimental jargon . . . a facile redundancy singularly incorrect: Jean-Jacques with a touch of a kitchenmaid of the 19th century."

One story which made the rounds in Paris society described Louis Philippe and Queen Victoria walking in the garden when:

with true French politeness, he offered her a peach. The Queen seemed rather embarrassed how to skin it, when Louis Philippe took a large clasp-knife from his pocket. "When a man has been a poor devil like myself, obliged to live upon forty *sous* a day, he always carries a knife. I might have dispensed with it for the last few years; still, I do not wish to lose the habit—one does not know what may happen," he said.

The memory of his earlier poverty-stricken circumstances during the days of the French Revolution was never far from the new king. Even with a personal royal income of £750,000, he was still capable of announcing to his chief minister, "I am telling you that my children will be wanting for bread!" He had been called by Paris (and in those days Paris made the political decisions for all of France) to be an ideal monarch; he was only capable of being father of a large family who looked upon the throne of France as a suitable means of earning a living. And there were many times when the price of that living seemed far too high for Louis. As he grumbled to one of his relatives: "The crown of France is too cold in winter, too warm in summer; the sceptre is too blunt as a weapon of defence or attack, it is too short as a stick to lean upon: a good felt hat and a strong umbrella are at all times more useful."

An Unsatisfactory Compromise

The ascension of Louis Philippe to the throne had been widely propagandized throughout France as an amalgam of love for the monarchy and love for republican principles. Louis early realized that the *bourgeoisie* had no lost love for the monarchy; he came to realize as well that the *bourgeoisie* was far more interested in its own economic position than in "liberty, fraternity, and equality." The Citizen King learned to hate the Marseillaise, serving as it did as the symbol for pretended republican enthusiasm. The Paris mobs always insisted that he join in the chorus whenever the old revolutionary hymn was sung in his presence. On occasion a mob of Parisians would sing the Marseillaise again and again beneath the windows of the king until the poor harassed man came out and joined them in sheer self-defense. Once, when one of his ministers expressed concern at the frequency with which the king was called upon to sing the Marseillaise, he murmured in reply, "Do not worry yourself, *Monsieur le Ministre;* I am only moving my lips; I have ceased to pronounce the words for many a day."

It seems that both sides to the bargain of a *bourgeois* monarchy, i.e., citizens and king, came to view the whole transaction with disgust. In the years of the July Monarchy, a play was actually staged in Paris that portrayed the "King of the Shopkeepers" giving the heir to the throne the following advice on the proper method for governing France:

Do not be misled by a parcel of theorists, who will tell you that the citizen-monarchy is based upon the sovereign will of the people, or upon the strict observance of the Charter; this is merely so much drivel from the political Rights or Lefts. In reality, it does not signify a jot whether France be free at home and feared and respected abroad, whether the throne be hedged round with republican institutions or supported by an hereditary peerage, whether the language of her statesmen be weighty and the deeds of her soldiers heroic. The citizen monarchy and the art of governing consist of but one thing—the capacity of the principal ruler for shaking hands with any and every ragamuffin and out-of-elbows brute he meets.

Whatever else may be said of Louis Philippe's reign, this experiment in republican monarchy, presided over by the *bourgeoisie,* seemed to satisfy no one—not the republicans, not the *bourgeoisie,* certainly not the monarch. The king came to detest the *bourgeoisie,* thinking them second-rate intellectually and resenting their alleged "admiration" of the "Citizen King." He once remarked, "I am like the fool between two stools, only I happen to be between the comfortably stuffed easy-chair of the *bourgeois* drawing room and the piece of furniture seated on which Louis XIV is said to have received the Dutch ambassadors." Louis Philippe had been isolated from both the nobility and the *bourgeoisie* by this shift of power to the middle class, thus giving France a government respected by no one, not even the king himself.

The result of this unsatisfactory experiment in *bourgeois* rule was a lapse of political interest and a totally colorless regime. As Tocqueville recalled the period:

No sooner had the Revolution of 1830 become an accomplished fact, than there ensued a great lull in political passion, a sort of general subsidence, accompanied by a rapid increase in public wealth. The particular spirit of the middle class became the general spirit of the government; it ruled the latter's foreign policy as well as affairs at home: an active, industrious spirit, often dishonorable, generally orderly, occasionally reckless through vanity or egoism, but timid by temperament, moderate in all things except in its love of ease and comfort, and last but not least mediocre. It was a spirit which, mingled with that of the people or of the aristocracy, can do wonders; but which, by itself, will never produce more than a government short of both virtue and greatness. Master of everything in a manner that no aristocracy has ever been or may ever hope to be, the middle class, when called upon to assume the government, took it up as an industrial enterprise; it entrenched itself behind its power, and before long, in their egoism, each of

its members thought much more of his private business than of
public affairs; of his personal enjoyment than of the greatness of the
nation.

Soon after the Revolution of 1830, for which Bastiat had
entertained such high hopes, he was named justice of the peace
for the canton of Mugron. He remained in this position and
continued his quiet, undisturbed life of study throughout most
of Louis Philippe's reign. Years later he would look back to
the years after 1830 as an unfortunate and rudderless interlude
during which France was sliding into a morass of socialism.
But that course of events had not yet become clear to Bastiat
or to France.

CHAPTER 3

Freedom of Exchange

You have left our village, and now you are in Paris, that
seething whirlpool. . . .

THE 1830s MARKED A CONTINUATION OF BASTIAT'S
peaceful country life. His 1831 appointment as Mugron's justice of the peace did little to alter his day-to-day existence.
Two years later he was elected to membership in the General
Council of Landes. He accepted even that small additional
responsibility with concern, fearing that this might alter the
quiet pattern of his days. Bastiat seemed determined to live
out his time as a scholarly gentleman-farmer in the south of
France.

Meanwhile, France gave the superficial impression of prosperity and progress. Railroads were stretching across the nation, messages zoomed by semaphore from point to point at
unheard-of speed for a pretelegraphic age. Louis Philippe's
chief minister, Guizot, had urged the middle classes to enrich
themselves, and the bourgeois Frenchmen were busily engaged
in that task. But not all was as cheerful and harmonious as it
appeared: during 1835, several attempts were made on the
King's life. For the next decade, Louis Philippe was periodi-
cally threatened. The unrest mirrored by these attempts was
aggravated by the government's repressive attitude toward the
press. Louis Philippe wanted to stop the publication of articles

that might incite insurrection or assassination. In practice, the royal edicts were often used to suppress all dissent. As a result, public opinion reflected in the popular press seemed almost totally complacent, but beneath the surface simmered widespread discontent.

Napoleon's nephew, Louis Napoleon, sought to capitalize on that discontent and crossed the Swiss border in 1836, entering Strasbourg and urging the city's inhabitants to rise in rebellion. Louis Philippe exported the would-be revolutionary to New York. Several years later, Louis Napoleon tried again to overthrow the French monarchy. This time he crossed the English Channel, bringing with him a tame eagle, presumably to remind the romantic French of his uncle's imperial eagles. Louis Philippe this time exiled the incurably ambitious revolutionary to a castle in Ham, a village in northern France. Though the exile was announced as a life sentence, within six years Louis Napoleon had again escaped to England where he bided his time and prepared for a third coup, which was ultimately to prove successful.

In the midst of so many trials, Louis Philippe leaned heavily on the *bourgeoisie* to maintain his position. Only the wealthier middle classes were allowed the vote. And to insure their support the monarchy granted them special privileges. The power of government was used freely to feather the nests of some citizens at the expense of others. The working classes, already excluded from the vote, grew restive in the face of this unfair division of government favors. Meanwhile, industrialism was having its impact on France. By 1840, one of every seven Frenchmen worked in the new manufacturing industries. Thus a growing proletariat comprised a new element in French society. In the regulated French economy, shortages of housing became the rule rather than the exception. These shortages, plus the exclusion of the working classes from the vote, formed a reservoir of discontent that was soon exploited by a number of theoreticians and would-be social philosophers who promised that true "equality" could be attained if only France would adopt their particular scheme. Worse still for the French people, most of these schemes were based upon a desire for greater and greater government planning and control.

Previously the upper middle class had blamed the nobility for France's problems—all France was to be prosperous once political power rested in solid bourgeois hands. However, when the upper middle classes achieved political power, they found themselves subject to the same criticism: "Louis Philippe and his *bourgeois* regime are responsible for all our problems; all France will be prosperous once political power rests safely in the hands of the lower middle classes and the workers!" As this new battle cry developed, the peasants sat back, watched the entire farce, and said nothing. Perhaps the peasants were wondering when their turn would come. Perhaps they were only amazed that the lust for political power could infect one class after another in precisely the same way.

Bastiat and the Tariff

One of the chief ways in which the *bourgeoisie* used political power to their own advantage and France's detriment was the tariff. As a member of a merchant family, Bastiat was especially sensitive to this issue. Thus it was the tariff which first caused him to question the uses of political power. In 1829 he had begun a study on the tariff and its injustices, but the Revolution of 1830 delayed printing for so long that the manuscript was never published.

Bastiat needed look no further than Bayonne, the city of his own career as a merchant, to see the harm done by trade regulations, restrictions and tariffs. A walk among the empty warehouses and along the silent docks was an education in itself. Tariffs in France had been raised repeatedly in the 19th century—always raised and never lowered to any real extent. For Bastiat, violations of the free trade principles of Say and Smith were the self-evident reason for the growing discontent of the French people.

In 1840 the gentleman farmer of Mugron decided to visit Spain and Portugal in the hope of establishing an insurance company. Since Bastiat was not distinguished for his interest in business affairs, it may well be that the trip was undertaken at least partially for its own sake. Though he traveled during the summer, he came down with a persistent illness that plagued him until he finally cut short his stay. But while in Madrid and Lisbon, Bastiat saw other nations making the same mistakes he had seen in France. In the process he developed a keen ear for ridiculous pro-tariff arguments. Later he described his impressions of the legislatures of Spain and Portugal:

Some years ago I was in Madrid where I attended a session of the Cortés. The subject under discussion was a treaty with Portugal for improving navigation on the Douro. One of the deputies rose and said: "If the Douro is canalized, shipping rates for cargoes traveling on it will be reduced. Portuguese grain will consequently sell at a lower price in the markets of Castile and will provide formidable competition for our domestic industry. I oppose the project, unless our cabinet ministers agree to raise the customs duty so as to redress the balance." The assembly found this argument unanswerable.

Three months later I was in Lisbon. The same question was up for discussion in the Senate. A great *hidalgo* said: "Mr. President, the project is absurd. At great cost you have set guards along the banks of the Douro to prevent an invasion of Portugal by Castilian grain, and at the same time you propose, again at great cost, to facilitate that invasion. It is an inconsistency to which I cannot assent. Let us leave the Douro to our children in just the same condition as our forefathers left it to us."

Bastiat never ceased to marvel at the excuses men would advance for destructive practices that limited trade. It appeared that men of Spain and Portugal were to be protected at all costs from the harmful effects of inexpensive and plentiful grain.

The French people also enjoyed similar "protection." The importation of grain and some other agricultural products was totally forbidden. Frenchmen were not allowed to import tea, since, in the language of a contemporary textbook, "this beverage affects the national character in giving the stern outlook of those men of the north, while wine denotes a soft gaiety." English iron and cloth were available at such low prices in the French market that, for the "protection" of the Frenchman, the July Monarchy was forced to institute steps that at first doubled the French price of English iron and cloth and finally forbade any further importation.

While the rural population of France thus found its standard of living somewhat reduced as the result of "protectionism," the living conditions in French cities were driven to unbelievably low levels. "Protected" prices were maintained at a level far too high for the wages of the time. In many cases, work was not available at any price. Of 150,000 residents of Lyon, 100,000 were described as indigent. By 1840 there were 130,000 abandoned children in the streets of French cities. It seemed clear to Bastiat that Frenchmen needed protection primarily from "protection." Government interference in freedom of transactions was stifling the French economy.

Bastiat had ventured to publish some of his thoughts on the tariff, primarily as applied to the French wine industry. In 1834, 1841, and 1843, his pieces had appeared in print, but with little or no public attention or comment. As late as the mid-1840s, it seemed that Bastiat was to remain the gentleman farmer with the dilettante's interest in public affairs. The turning point in his life came quite by chance.

At a time when anti-British feeling ran high in France, Bastiat's open-minded attitudes often made him the target for criticism among his friends when the subject of England arose. It arose one day with a vengeance in a Mugron discussion group to which Bastiat belonged. A French newspaper had quoted the British Prime Minister, speaking in opposition to a proposed measure, as saying that, if the measure in question were adopted, ". . . we will become, like France, a second-class nation." Bastiat's friends were incensed, and, as usual, turned to him as though he and "his British friends" were personally responsible for this insult.

Typically, Bastiat checked his facts before saying a word. He ordered back issues of *The Globe* and *Traveler* to check Prime Minister Peel's speech in an English version, discovering that the phrase, "like France" had been maliciously inserted in the French version by an Anglophobe translator. Bastiat won his argument; more important, he discovered the Anti-Corn Law League and the free trade work of Richard Cobden. French newspapers had paid virtually no attention to the English free trade movement. The news that like-minded believers in freedom of transactions were engaged in a widespread campaign to bring free trade to a neighboring country brought a breath of excitement to Bastiat's life. From that day forward, Frederic Bastiat closely followed the work of Richard

Cobden and the development of the free trade movement in England.

Cobden and the League

Richard Cobden was more French than English in his philosophic views. He drew his ideas from the 18th century and based his social thought on the assumption that human nature was perfectible. In this, Cobden was far closer to the French *philosophes* than Bastiat would ever be. Yet Bastiat would base his leadership of the French free trade movement almost entirely upon the ideas and organizational principles of his English mentor. Cobden had organized a splendid vehicle for the propagation of the free trade idea. Free trade speakers were on the hustings everywhere in England. Handbills and posters confronted Englishmen at every turn. Cobden and his most brilliant associate, John Bright, developed such a reputation for invincibility that soon parliamentary opponents of free trade were unwilling to appear against them on the debate platform. As historian Dean Russell observed, "It is almost certain that there was not even one literate person in all of Great Britain who had not read of the League and its work by the end of 1844."

Certainly Frederic Bastiat was deeply involved in the whole tariff question by the end of 1844. In the white heat of excitement generated by Cobden and his crusade, Bastiat produced by far his most notable writing to that date, a study of the influences of English and French tariffs on the future of the two countries. He submitted the piece to the prestigious *Journal des économistes,* painfully aware that several pieces he had written in the early 1840s had never found a publisher.

The editors examined this article by an unknown author from the provinces and realized that they had discovered a brilliant new economic thinker with a fresh analysis of the problems plaguing French society. The article was published in October 1844, and overnight Frederic Bastiat found himself an established author. Compliments poured into Mugron, together with requests for more articles. Bastiat immediately began contributing further to the *Journal* and also began gathering material for a history of Cobden's Anti-Corn Law League. The correspondence with Cobden continued for the remainder of Bastiat's life.

From the time of the first article's publication in the *Journal des économistes,* Bastiat was launched upon a new career and a new phase of his life. The articles which he now began to pour out for publication in various journals would soon be published as *Economic Sophisms.* He was elected a corresponding member of the French Academy of Science. Mugron could not hold its gentleman farmer much longer.

Bastiat had spent years qualifying to be called, and now the call had come. A genuine modesty and an unwillingness to leave his quiet, contemplative life caused him to delay for a time the enormous changes about to occur in his existence. He remained in Mugron to complete his book on Cobden and the English free trade movement.

At last Bastiat went to Paris in May 1845 to make publication arrangements for his book on Cobden. By July, he was on his way to England to meet the leaders of the free trade movement. He left Paris in triumph, with offers to direct the *Journal des économistes* and with suggestions that he should assume a university chair in political economy. The long years of reading and conversation with Coudroy now stood him in good stead. Paris found him a brilliant conversationalist as well as a fine writer. Bastiat was not a great orator, but with small groups of interested people, he was in his element. Perhaps his lifelong habits of study and concentration had convinced him that large audiences seldom retain anything of lasting value. At any rate, he generally seemed to act on the principle that "the best audience is an audience of one."

The same flair for direct and highly individualized communication was also readily apparent in his writing. Returning to Mugron, he wrote easily and rapidly as twenty years of concentrated study and thought poured out of his mind and heart. *Economic Sophisms* had appeared in its first edition before the end of 1845; *Economic Harmonies* and many of his other essays also would soon find their way into print.

The Debate Begins

As Bastiat's fame spread and his arguments favoring free trade appeared in various newspapers and pamphlets throughout France, he immediately became the target for numerous public attacks. He was accused of pro-English sentiment because of his connections with Cobden and the League. This charge carried great weight in an age which found most Frenchmen actively hostile to anything English. Also, workers were told that Bastiat's ideas would lead to unemployment and starvation for the working classes. Every half-truth and falsehood imaginable was trotted out by the opponents of free trade.

Bastiat set a pattern which proponents of freedom could well follow in any age. He kept his temper and published refutations of the entire protectionist position, demolishing his opposition with simple language and easily understood examples. Throughout, Bastiat reflected a sense of humor which illuminated the foibles of his age and which made the hard facts and tight logical analysis of his position far more popular and palatable than the usual grim preaching by reformers.

Writing in his Mugron study far from Paris, Bastiat returned to his central themes again and again: the myth of "overproduction"; emphasis upon the interests of the consumer (reminding his readers that we are all consumers); and special emphasis upon the idea that a fundamental harmony pervades the free marketplace. Bastiat thus popularized the idea of Say and Smith that problems and distortions enter the economic scene as soon as government interference becomes the dominant force.

Building on the latter, Bastiat stressed that free exchange permitted a division of labor, "which makes it possible for each man, instead of struggling on his own behalf to overcome all the obstacles that stand in his way, to struggle against only one, not solely on his own account, but for the benefit of his fellow men, who in turn perform the same service for him."

Thus, specialization leads to increased production, of those items most desired by consumers, at a price which the consumers themselves are willing to pay. In free exchange, then, a natural harmony exists between production and consumption, between specialists and consumers of the specialty, provided only that the system is allowed to operate. The system, as Bastiat made clear again and again, can operate only so long as voluntary association and free choice prevail. The harmony of mutual interest is destroyed when the outside agency of the state introduces compulsion in place of voluntary cooperation. As Bastiat wrote:

For a man, when he gets up in the morning, to be able to put on a suit of clothes, a piece of land has had to be enclosed, fertilized, drained, cultivated, planted with a certain kind of vegetation; flocks of sheep have had to feed on it; they have had to give their wool; this wool has had to be spun, woven, dyed, and converted into cloth; this cloth has had to be cut, sewn, and fashioned into a garment. And this series of operations implies a host of others; for it presupposes the use of farming implements, of sheepfolds, of factories, of coal, of machines, of carriages, etc.

If society were not a very real association, anyone who wanted a suit of clothes would be reduced to working in isolation, that is, to performing himself the innumerable operations in this series, from the first blow of the pickaxe that initiates it right down to the last thrust of the needle that terminates it.

But thanks to that readiness to associate which is the distinctive characteristic of our species, these operations have been distributed among a multitude of workers, and they keep subdividing themselves more and more for the common good to the point where, as consumption increases, a single specialized operation can support a new industry. Then comes the distribution of the proceeds, according to the portion of value each one has contributed to the total work. If this is not association, I should like to know what is.

Do not this division of labor and these arrangements, decided upon in full liberty, serve the common good? Do we, then, need a socialist, under the pretext of planning, to come and despotically destroy our voluntary arrangements, put an end to the division of labor, substitute isolated efforts for co-operative efforts, and reverse the progress of civilization?

Though Bastiat's return to the peace and quiet of Mugron had given him an ideal opportunity to produce a steady flow of essays, he had been troubled by the feeling that still more needed to be done. There persisted in his thoughts the idea that a French free trade movement patterned on Cobden's work in England was an absolute necessity before freedom of transactions could be brought to France.

However effective Bastiat had now proven himself as a writer and thinker, nothing in the quiet young man's life had shown that he had the slightest flair for organization or for public life. But once again events were destined to redirect the life of Frederic Bastiat. A Bordeaux trade association had decided to petition the government for a Belgian-French customs union. Attracted by Bastiat's growing reputation as a foe of tariff barriers, the group in question asked for his help in their campaign. Bastiat eagerly accepted. He wrote articles for the Bordeaux newspaper and made a series of speeches in which he soon turned the issue from the limited question of a customs union with one nation to the broader issue of free trade with all nations. By early 1846, the Bordeaux Association for Free Trade had become a reality.

The French Free Trade Association

Bastiat decided that the time had come for a nationwide free trade association. Fresh from his triumph in Bordeaux, he went to Paris to form an organization based on the Cobden model. The young author began to arrange a series of meetings, publish pamphlets and flyers, undertake speaking tours, and organize affiliate free trade associations in key French cities. He found his ambitious undertaking to be far more difficult than he had believed in his first enthusiasm. Writing to his old friend, Coudroy, Bastiat complained, "I am losing all my time, the association is progressing at a turtle's pace." Finding metropolitan Paris a tough nut to crack without wealth and position, he wrote his new friend, Richard Cobden: "I feel that this superb Babylon is not my place and that it is necessary that I hasten to return to my solitude." But Bastiat eventually decided to stay in Paris, on the firing line where the issues were being debated.

One of the key figures in Bastiat's decision to stay was

Michel Chevalier. A member of the Society of Economists and influential in the publication of the *Journal des débats,* Chevalier had been much impressed with Bastiat's writing and had urged him to come to Paris. He was to become a close associate in the struggle to found a national free trade association.

During the spring of 1846, Bastiat and the group which formed around him in Paris met to hammer out a "Declaration of Principles" and to perfect their organizational plans. On May 4, Bastiat was named director. The group had high hopes for the new organization, believing that free trade was both an important step toward securing other freedoms for the individual and a vital step toward ending war: "When goods don't cross borders, armies will." From the beginning, the group stressed that material benefits would come to the typical Frenchman as the result of free trade, but always insisted upon the broader moral point that peace and freedom were the really significant goals of the free trade movement.

The French government delayed for several months the issuance of formal authorization to the free-trade group, but Bastiat was coming to understand the workings of French politics more each day. He finally wrote a letter to a government minister, Duchatel, containing the correct balance of supplication and inside information. The letter provided the needed leverage, and the French Free Trade Association was granted government approval for its activities, despite the resistance of the protectionist lobbyists who exercised so much influence in the French government of the 1840s.

The great significance of political leverage was becoming clear to Bastiat as he became more acquainted with Parisian society. He even thought for a time that he might enter national politics in 1846, and he prepared a campaign brochure for the electors of his home district around Mugron. He was not nominated. Engrossed with his lectures, his writing and his attempts to organize the trade association, he was far too independent in his views and disinterested in the influence peddling that characterized French politics in the July Monarchy to undertake a serious political campaign.

Michel Chevalier also was unsuccessful in the 1846 elections, losing his bid for re-election in his home district. He and Bastiat returned to Paris where the Association held an August dinner for Cobden. This dinner marked the climax of efforts to organize the group. With politics out of the way for the moment, the Association was about to launch a concerted campaign of public meetings and educational publications. The first public meeting was held August 28. Bringing together groups of legislators and key figures from the French world of affairs, Bastiat's group held several meetings during the fall of 1846. Public interest was keen, with turn-away crowds at each meeting numbering over 2,000. Soon Le Havre and Marseilles had followed the lead of Bordeaux and Paris in the formation of free trade associations. Meetings continued during 1847 and the early months of 1848. Bastiat and his friends had high hopes that they were on the road to as great a free trade triumph in France as Richard Cobden had achieved in England.

"The Petition of the Candlemakers"

Bastiat had concentrated from the beginning upon attracting favorable publicity to the issue of free trade. Aglow with success, he wrote Cobden, "Unquestionably, we are making progress. Six months ago, we didn't have even one newspaper for us. Today we have five in Paris, three in Bordeaux, two in Marseilles, one in Le Havre, and two in Bayonne." However, he came to realize as time passed that a newspaper devoted to free trade, published in Paris by the Association itself, would be a great asset. On November 29, 1846, the first issue of *Le libre-échange* was published under Bastiat's editorship. Here is his famous "Petition of the Candlemakers," which appeared in the pages of this new publication:

From the Manufacturers of Candles, Tapers, Lanterns, Candlesticks, Street Lamps, Snuffers, and Extinguishers, and from the Producers of Tallow, Oil, Resin, Alcohol, and Generally Everything Connected with Lighting.

To the Honorable Members of the Chamber of Deputies

Gentlemen:

We are suffering from the ruinous competition of a foreign rival who apparently works under conditions so far superior to our own for the production of light that he is flooding the domestic market with it at an incredibly low price; from the moment he appears, our sales cease, all the consumers turn to him, and a branch of French industry whose ramifications are innumerable is all at once reduced to complete stagnation. This rival, which is none other than the sun, is waging war on us so mercilessly that we suspect he is being stirred up against us by perfidious Albion [England] (excellent diplomacy nowadays!), particularly because he has for that haughty island a respect that he does not show for us.

We ask you to be so good as to pass a law requiring the closing of all windows, dormers, skylights, inside and outside shutters, curtains, casements, bull's eyes, deadlights, and blinds—in short, all openings, holes, chinks, and fissures through which the light of the sun is wont to enter houses, to the detriment of the fair industries with which, we are proud to say, we have endowed the country, a country that cannot, without betraying ingratitude, abandon us today to so unequal a combat. . . .

Bastiat also drove home the point in another way:

When a product—coal, iron, wheat, or textiles—comes to us from abroad, and when we can acquire it for less labor than if we produced it ourselves, the difference is a *gratuitous gift* that is conferred upon us. The size of this gift is proportionate to the extent of this difference. It is a quarter, a half, or three-quarters of the value of the product if the foreigner asks of us only three-quarters, one-half, or one-quarter as high a price. It is as complete as it can be when the donor, like the sun in providing us with light, asks nothing from us. The question, and we pose it formally, is whether what you desire for France is the benefit of consumption free of charge or the alleged advantages of onerous production.

Bastiat never tired of attacking the notion that France could become rich by retarding production. In the September 18, 1846 issue of *Courier français,* he wrote, again in a satirical vein, a letter to the king:

> . . . there will be formed an association *in defense of labor with the left hand,* and the advocates of *left-hand labor* will have no trouble demolishing all these generalities, speculations, assumptions, abstractions, reveries, and utopian fantasies. They will need only to exhume the *Moniteur industriel* [a protectionist newspaper] of 1846; they will find ready-made arguments against freedom of trade that will do quite well as against *freedom for the right hand* if they will merely substitute one expression for the other. . . . The old system of *restriction* was based on the idea of creating obstacles in order to multiply job opportunities. The new system of *restriction* that we are proposing to take its place is based on exactly the same idea. Sire, to make laws in this fashion is not to innovate; it is to carry on in the traditional way.
>
> As for the efficacy of the measure, it is uncontestable. It is difficult, much more difficult than people think, to do with the left hand what one is accustomed to doing with the right. You will be convinced of this, Sire, if you will deign to put our system to the test in performing some act that is familiar to you, such as, for instance, that of shuffling cards. We can, therefore, flatter

ourselves on opening to labor an unlimited number of job opportunities.

Once the workers in every branch of industry are restricted to the use of their left hands alone, imagine, Sire, the immense number of people that will be needed to meet the present demand for consumer goods, assuming that it remains constant, as we always do when we compare different systems of production. So prodigious a demand for manual labor cannot fail to bring about a considerable rise in wages, and pauperism will disappear from the country as if by magic.

During the same period, Bastiat published a piece in the *Journal des économistes* entitled "Robbery by Subsidy":

Now, does the monopolist who, by means of a law of his own making, makes it necessary for me to pay him twenty francs for what I could buy elsewhere for fifteen, take from me, by fraud, five francs that belong to me?

Does he not appropriate them by *stealth* or *force?*

Does he not exact more than his due?

He does, indeed, it may be said, take; he does appropriate; he does exact; but not at all by stealth or force, which are characteristics of robbery.

When our tax accounts contain a charge of five francs for the subsidy that the monopolist takes, appropriates, or exacts, what could be more *stealthy,* since so few of us suspect it? And for those who are not dupes, what could be more *forced,* since at the first sign of refusal, the bailiff's man is at our door?

Still, the monopolists need have no anxiety on that score. Robberies *by subsidy* or *by tariff,* though they violate equity quite as much as highway robbery does, do not violate the law; on the contrary, they are perpetrated by means of the law; this fact only makes them worse, but the *magistrates* have no quarrel with them.

Bastiat's clever irony was much appreciated. His writing became as popular with the general reading public as it was hated by the protectionists. During the second year of the French Free Trade Association, the free trade movement was taking on international status. Similar associations were springing up in Spain, Italy, Belgium, Sweden, and Germany. But the free trade movement in France was going in the opposite direction by 1847. Broad support was never achieved, and the French Free Trade Association ceased to exist in early 1848.

The Political Significance of Free Trade

Despite the setbacks for the free trade movement, Bastiat had already scored a signal victory. He was the first to sense and write about the vital nature of the *total* question posed by human freedom. At the height of the free trade movement, he wrote to Cobden, "Rather than the fact of free trade alone, I desire for my country the general philosophy of free trade. While free trade will bring more wealth to us, the acceptance of the general philosophy that underlies free trade will inspire all needed reforms." In a note to himself, he added, "All forms of freedom are interrelated. Together they constitute a systematic and harmonious whole; there is not one of them that, when proved true, would not help to prove the truth of the others. But [I] am acting like a mechanic who is taking the utmost pains to explain an isolated piece of machinery down to its most minute detail. . . ."

The problem of injustice was actually the central feature of Bastiat's argument. In *Economic Sophisms,* he described a compelling picture:

> I enter one of the cottages that cling to the French side of the Pyrénées.

The head of the family receives only a slender wage for his work. His half-naked children shiver in the icy north wind; the fire is out, and there is nothing on the table. On the other side of the mountain there are wool, firewood, and corn; but these products are forbidden to the family of the poor day-laborer, for the other side of the mountain is not in France. Foreign spruce will not gladden the cottage hearth; the shepherd's children will not know the taste of Biscayan muslin; and the wool from Navarre will never warm their numbed limbs. All this is, we are told, in the interest of the general welfare. Very well. But then it must be admitted that in this instance the general welfare is in conflict with justice.

To regulate the consumers by law and limit them to the products of domestic industry is to encroach upon their freedom by forbidding them an action—exchange—that in itself is in no way contrary to morality; in short, it is to do them an *injustice.*

And yet, we are told, this is necessary if production is to be maintained and the prosperity of the country is not to receive a fatal blow.

The writers of the protectionist school thus reach the melancholy conclusion that there is a radical incompatibility between justice and the general welfare.

For Bastiat, of course, no such incompatibility could exist. The "general welfare" protectionists and other special interests were calling upon to rationalize and legitimize restricting the political and economic rights of citizens was illusory. He realized then that free trade was part of a larger issue: freedom in all human activity. What truly set him apart from his contemporaries was his instance that government, no matter in whose interests it was run, can only be a harmful force when it sacrifices specific, enumerated individual rights in the name of an arbitrary, ill-defined "greater good." At 30, Bastiat believed that middle-class government could control and direct France. At 45, he knew that a government bent on managing human affairs could not ensure justice or freedom.

CHAPTER 4

Revolution: February 1848

We have tried so many things; when shall we try the simplest of all: freedom?

THE INDUSTRIAL DEVELOPMENT OF FRANCE OC-curred under peculiarly trying circumstances during the 1840s. At best, an era of major transition brings with it dislocation of many sorts, but the Frenchmen of Bastiat's generation found themselves faced with more than an era of rapid change. They were also faced with a government determined to regulate and manipulate society. Those who were most sensitive to the current of affairs in France soon perceived that any truly independent business enterprise was likely to run disastrously afoul of the French government and its complicated, contradictory legalisms. A far more promising road to success seemed to lie through politically oriented business dealings. How much easier it seemed to run a business supported by a government tariff, a government monopoly or even government capital.

If the productive businessman suffered under such a regime, the growing French proletariat suffered far more deeply. Real wages, what the paycheck of the French worker would actually buy at the grocery store, had been declining steadily since 1820. Prosperity seemed reserved for the few *bourgeoisie* who knew how to make government serve their purposes. There had been serious strikes during 1831–1832, and again in 1833, followed by the general strike of 1840. As the 1840s wore on, the picture grew even darker. Bad harvests in 1845 and 1846 had driven food prices ever higher. A severe industrial depression began in 1847, causing such widespread unemployment that over one-third of the population of Paris was on relief before the end of the year. At the very height of this distress, a cholera epidemic swept the city.

The French people would gladly have turned to anyone who offered relief in their time of distress, but they received only the shabbiest of platitudes and the most ridiculous analyses of their troubles. One member of the Chamber of Deputies received standing applause when he proposed that the depression of 1847 was due primarily to "external weakness" and "idle pacifism." It seemed that the troubles of France were due to an insufficiently militant foreign policy. While the Chamber of Deputies pondered the lost glories of French militarism, business after business failed throughout France. The number of businesses in Paris declined by over fifty percent during 1848.

The Corruption of French Society

The King's first minister during the crisis of the 1840s was François Guizot. He remained firmly convinced that France would prosper so long as only the wealthier members of the middle class had the right of suffrage. Provided the right people were running the government, surely the citizens of France need not worry. A few years earlier, Guizot had advised all Frenchmen to join the wealthy middle classes: *"Enrichissez vous, enrichissez vous."* Oddly enough, Guizot's private life was an absolute model of puritan rectitude, so out of character for

the France of his time that even Louis Philippe had once remarked of his chief minister, "Guizot is so terribly respectable;
I am afraid there is a mistake either about his nationality or
his respectability, for they are badly matched."

However respectable Guizot was in his private life, he presided over an era in which prosperity was assumed to be found
through courting the special privileges of government. The
corruption implicit in such a system had spread throughout
French society. As Priscilla Robertson, one historian of the
period, has described it:

> The answer of the government to its growing unpopularity was
> corruption. If it could not placate the majority of the people be-
> cause it did not trust them, it could at least control its own minor-
> ity by bribes. Its candidates were returned to the Chamber by
> promises of bridges, railroads, and hospitals to doubtful districts—
> a practice which led, incidentally, to an extraordinarily spotty
> development of railroad connections in those first years when they
> were being pushed through. Another common favor was the issu-
> ance of pardons or of exemptions from military service. Public
> morals sank below any recent remembrance. The director of the
> military bakery used state funds to speculate in wheat, leaving a
> tremendous deficit at his death. Two peers of France were actually
> tried and sentenced for dishonesty in a mining concession, and the
> case might never have come to trial if the principals had not quar-
> reled and one published the other's incriminating letters. But the
> climax was the *"affaire Petit,"* when Guizot himself, hitherto felt
> to be a rock of personal honesty, was shown to have paid 60,000
> francs out of secret service money to recompense a man who had
> bought a place in the bureau of auditing and then not received the
> post.

Since the *bourgeoisie* had displayed such well-publicized and
self-congratulatory rectitude in their assurances to the people
of France that middle class control would be best for all, it is

not surprising that the *bourgeoisie,* indeed, all men of property, became the hated scapegoats for Frenchmen in their hour of troubles. One cartoon of the times shows a dissipated loafer leaning against a lamp post, contemptuously eyeing a well-dressed *bourgeois* out for his Sunday stroll with his wife.

The loafer is smoking a short, clay pipe, some of the fumes of which drift into the path of the *bourgeois* family and apparently offend their respectability. The *bourgeois* turns to the loafer, saying, "Begone!"

"It is time for you to be gone, you pig!" replies the Parisian man-of-the-streets. And there can be little doubt that it was an accurate expression of popular sentiment in 1848. While hatreds mounted, the debates of the Chamber of Deputies seemed an exercise in futility. One of the deputies later wrote that "these great orators were bored to death at listening to one another, and, what was worse, the whole country was bored with listening to them. France grew unconsciously accustomed to look upon the debates in the Chamber as exercises of the intellect rather than as serious discussions."

The government, meanwhile, seemed blissfully unaware that not all was well in France. Corruption entered government dealings, and thence in turn corrupted all aspects of French life. Dishonesty became the order of the day for all classes. Complaints of false weights and adulteration made even minor transactions almost impossible. French wines were so often adulterated that they became difficult to sell abroad.

Perhaps those members of the Chamber of Deputies who blamed all of France's troubles on an insufficiently militant foreign policy were less stupid than they would appear at first glance. Their analysis of France's afflictions may have been woefully inadequate; but their knowledge of French psychology was right on the mark. A young journalist about to make a name for himself in the rapidly approaching revolution, Louis Blanc, expressed the sentiment of the typical Frenchman when he complained that France was a nation of warriors doomed to impotence because it was governed by the petty, shopkeeping *bourgeoisie.* The poor people of Paris were always jingoes. No matter how much Louis Philippe's innocuous foreign policy might have appealed to his fellow European monarchs, it left much to be desired in the hearts of French workers and students. The French poor suffered a miserable present, but they remembered the glorious days of the Empire, when all the world had waited with baited breath to see what the next move of Napoleon I would be. The lunatic fringe of Paris had made 17 assassination attempts on King Louis Philippe since 1830; and Richard Rush, the American minister to France, felt that the reason for these attempts at assassination had centered primarily on the fact that Louis Philippe had wanted peace for for his homeland.

Since Louis Philippe had been on the throne, France had acquiesced in treaties which involved the loss of Nice and Savoy to the south, plus an unfavorable change in the Rhine frontier to the east. The people of France hated the *bourgeois* July Monarchy even more for France's lost glory than for her hard times. Some of the nation's most wily demagogues were not above playing upon this fact of French politics for all it was worth. By 1848, discontent with the July Monarchy had reached such feverish intensity that some radical change seemed unavoidable.

On the Eve of Revolution

The last days of the July Monarchy were also the exciting and busy days that saw Bastiat's development of the free trade movement. He was publishing a weekly newspaper, speaking at meetings, corresponding with new free trade associations which were forming in the provinces, writing letters and controversial articles in three different journals, and also doing some of the writing which would later prove his most lasting monument. He worked feverishly night and day. In the midst of all his other labors, Bastiat found time to visit Cobden, Bright and the other key figures in the English free trade movement and to deliver a series of lectures on political economy to a group of young Parisian students. And he struggled with a steadily weakening health. He had contracted tuberculosis, but was unwilling to slow the pace of his work long enough to take a much-needed rest. But the events of February 1848 put an end to Bastiat's teaching and an end to all hopes of further free trade activity in France.

From that time on, events were to move so rapidly that Bastiat had to take quite another line of defense. On the eve of the February 1848 revolution, Bastiat found himself living in a radically inflammatory and totally corrupt Paris. As the British author Thackeray described the city after his visit during those days, "Everything here seemed to me to be ranting, gaudy and theatrical. Fictional liberty, fictional monarchy, fictional glory, fictional justice." Paris was in a state of ferment, a home for the ambitious, the malcontents, the political failures, the wild-eyed visionaries.

Since the stormy days of 1789, Europe had looked to France as the home of revolutions. Based on performance, there was some justice in that reputation. It is also true that of the major European capitals, only Paris possessed a working class sufficiently organized to carry out an effective uprising.

Much of the working class organization was due to the efforts of Louis Blanc, a bitter foe of the July Monarchy. Blanc was willing to use force to achieve his ends, but was far from the most radical Frenchman in the Paris of 1848. Such men as Armand Barbès and Auguste Blanqui were far more bloodthirsty. They labored ceaselessly to build effective secret societies committed to "washing in the blood of kings." In 1839, both Barbès and Blanqui had been sentenced to death in the aftermath of an aborted coup. Under pressure from Victor Hugo, the always gentle Louis Philippe had commuted the sentences. Thus Barbès and Blanqui were ready to come out of prison and renew their agitation at the moment the monarchy tottered and fell.

The signal of the impending fall was clearly sounded in southern France on July 18, 1847. The town of Mâcon had arranged a banquet for its favorite son, the distinguished poet and historian, Alphonse de Lamartine. The banquet was spread outdoors and the banqueters found themselves drenched in a heavy summer thunder shower at the very moment when Lamartine was to begin speaking. But Lamartine's speech was such that no one of the 6,000 people attending the affair so much as stirred in his seat:

> It will fall, this royalty, be sure of that. It will fall, not in its blood like that of 1789; but it will fall in its trap. And after having had the revolution of freedom and the counter-revolution of glory, you will have the revolution of public conscience and the Revolution of Contempt.

In Lamartine's phrase, "the Revolution of Contempt," the Revolution of 1848 is epitomized. The July Monarchy fell less because it was overthrown than because no one was willing to support it any longer.

By the end of 1847, the custom of political banquets was

well established throughout France. The mere act of buying a ticket for one of these banquets became symbolic of member-ship in the Revolution of Contempt. The banquets became a vehicle for a more moderate expression of discontent, involving responsible politicians as well as radical revolutionaries. Soon such events forced the government of Louis Philippe to take stronger action. One of the largest and most popular of the banquets was scheduled for Paris in February 1848. Goaded by the abuses of the opposition, the government decided that the banquet must be banned. This was the signal for which Paris had been waiting. With cries of "Long live the Repub-lic!" the workers and the students poured into the streets, erecting barricades and waving the red flag. Fires were started all over the city. Soon, troops were ordered to shoot arsonists on sight.

The Indecision of Politicians

Fanaticism reached a fever pitch. One worker who anticipated the revolution walked about the streets carrying multiple loaves of bread beneath his arm, explaining, "For the three days; we always do such things in three days." It was soon obvious that the people of Paris were considerably ahead of their leadership. The organizers of the political banquets now found themselves astride a tiger that was increasingly difficult to ride. Most of the political figures organizing the banquets had never intended the note of violence that was now every-where in the air. Meanwhile, the leaderless people of Paris continued fanning their own revolutionary fervor. Lamartine could only stand by indecisively and wring his hands, believ-ing that the people did not want Louis Blanc's socialism. Louis Blanc could only talk endlessly of how the people wanted more than Lamartine's republic. Neither could believe that anyone might follow a really radical revolutionary like Blanqui.

If the opposition politicians no longer knew where France was going, some observers saw the future course of events with painful accuracy. One of these was the young Alexis de Tocqueville, then a member of the Chamber of Deputies. Addressing the Chamber on the 29th of January 1848, Tocqueville warned:

> Do you not see that they [the people] are gradually forming opinions and ideas that are destined not only to upset this or that law, ministry, or even form of government, but society itself, until it totters upon the foundations on which it rests today? Do you not listen to what they say to themselves each day? Do you not hear them repeating unceasingly that all that is above them is incapable and unworthy of governing them; that the distribution of goods prevalent until now throughout the world is unjust; that property rests on a foundation that is not an equitable one? And do you not realize that when such opinions take root, when they spread in an almost universal manner, when they sink deeply into the masses, they are bound to bring with them sooner or later ... a most formidable revolution?
>
> This, gentlemen, is my profound conviction: I believe that we are at this moment sleeping on a volcano. I am profoundly convinced of it. . . .

Louis Philippe's first minister, Guizot, became the focal point around which the storm center formed. The people on the barricades were calling for his immediate dismissal from the government. It is said that Louis Philippe had tears in his eyes as he embraced his minister, but that he could hear the cries outside the palace window which convinced him that Guizot must go. Guizot walked through the streets to the Chamber of Deputies, a rash and brave act in itself. With his face pale and his head held high, he personally announced that he had been dismissed from the government.

If Louis Philippe had really believed that concessions to the mob would appease the revolutionary fervor of the people, he was sadly mistaken. Immediately after Guizot's dismissal, affairs lapsed into worse disorder than before. Louis Philippe seemed unable to take decisive action. Delessert, Louis' minister of police, urged that action must be taken soon, but was unable to find anyone in authority willing to take the responsibility for giving the order to move against the political enemies of the monarchy. Meanwhile, young revolutionaries were racing from barricade to barricade, insisting that the fall of Guizot was not enough and that the workers should march directly to the Chamber of Deputies and demand their full revolutionary rights.

In the midst of the growing crisis, the Chamber of Deputies sat in a state of suspended animation. They seemed afraid to voice any mention of the dark forebodings that hung over them. Guizot's appearance to announce his dismissal as the first minister of France interrupted a languid debate concerning a bill for the creation of a bank in Bordeaux. Guizot's dismissal at last forced them to face the issue. Alexis de Tocqueville painted a moving picture of that scene:

> The Opposition kept their seats, most of them uttering cries of victory and satisfied revenge; the leaders alone sat silent, busy in communing with themselves upon the use they would make of their triumph, and careful not to insult a majority of which they might soon be called upon to make use. As to the majority, they seemed thunderstruck by this so unexpected blow, moved to and fro like a mass that sways from side to side, uncertain as to which side it shall fall on, and then descended noisily into the semi-circle. A few surrounded the ministers to ask them for explanations or to

pay them their last respects, but the greater number clamored against them with noisy and insulting shouts. "To throw up office, to abandon your political friends under such circumstances," they said, "is a piece of gross cowardice"; while others exclaimed that the members ought to proceed to the Tuileries in a body and force the King to reconsider this fatal resolve.

This despair will arouse no astonishment when it is remembered that the greater number of these men felt themselves attacked not only in their political opinions, but in the most sensitive part of their private interest. The fall of the Government compromised the entire fortune of one, the daughter's dowry of another, the son's career of a third. It was by this that they were almost all held. Most of them had not only bettered themselves by means of their votes, but one may say that they had lived on them. They still lived on them, and hoped to continue to live on them; for, the Ministry having lasted eight years, they had accustomed themselves to think that it would last for ever; they had grown attached to it with the honest, peaceful feeling of affection which one entertains for one's fields. From my seat, I watched this swaying crowd; I saw surprise, anger, fear, and avarice mingle their various expressions upon those bewildered countenances; and I drew an involuntary comparison between all these legislators and a pack of hounds which with their jaws half filled, see the quarry withdrawn from them.

Tocqueville went on to put his finger upon the reason for the 1848 revolution, indeed, one of the prime reasons for the failure of many governments during the past two centuries:

I grant, however, that, so far as many of the Opposition were concerned, it only wanted that they should be put to a similar test in order to make the same display. If many of the Conservatives only defended the Ministry with a view to keeping their places and emoluments, I am bound to say that many of the Opposition seemed to me only to attack it in order to reap the plunder in their turn. The truth—the deplorable truth—is that a taste for holding office and a desire to live on the public money is not with us a disease restricted to either party, but the great, chronic ailment of the whole nation; the result of the democratic constitution of our society and of the excessive centralization of our Government; the secret malady that undermined all former governments and that will undermine all governments to come.

As the Chamber of Deputies continued to waver indecisively, the people moved to take power into their own hands. Bit by bit the Chamber began to fill with people from the streets of Paris. Many of them were armed. Soon the deputies found themselves surrounded by revolutionary rabble who stood by eyeing the lawmakers of France. Their silence was more pregnant with meaning than the wildest of outcries.

If the deputies were uneasy, they were probably no more uneasy than the revolutionary chieftains who were now called upon to take the next steps. While the Chamber of Deputies sat in the midst of the vast Parisian mob, the revolutionary leaders met at the Hotel de Ville in an effort to hammer out a provisional government. Lamartine was becoming the man of the hour by virtue of his impassioned oratory. Soon the dwarf, Louis Blanc, borne aloft on the shoulders of workers, forced his way into the discussions. Ouside the hotel the streets were filled with the wounded from the early fighting, with victims lying on blood-soaked straw pallets. Every café and every meeting place was jammed with gesticulating students, workers and intellectuals.

Middle Class Apathy and Violence in the Streets

As larger and larger crowds milled aimlessly about the streets of Paris, all responsibility for policing the city fell upon the National Guard. The middle class National Guardsmen were unwilling to face any serious possibility of putting down the revolution. While it is true that most of the Guard probably did not want a republic, their failure to decisively support the monarchy led inevitably to the fall of Louis Philippe. To compound the confusion, rumors spread through the streets that the government was massacring the poor. The middle class kept insisting to itself, amidst great quantities of hand wringing, "It is the government's fault, let the government solve its own problems. Why should we get killed for people who have managed their business so badly?"

And yet in Tocqueville's sharp appraisal, "this was that middle class that had been pampered for eighteen years: the current of public opinion had ended by dragging it along, and it was driving it against those who had flattered it until it had become corrupt."

Soon the National Guardsmen were stacking their muskets and fraternizing with the crowd. Paris was without public authority: not a single soldier, nor a policeman remained in authority. The people filled the streets, gave the orders, and served as judge, jury, and executioner. Louis Philippe put in a brave public appearance or two in the vicinity of the Tuileries, but it was obvious that he rallied no support from any segment of society. The crowds around the Tuileries grew so immense and impassioned that many suffocated. Within a few hours, a broken Louis Philippe slipped out of Paris, never to return.

With the departure of the King, casualties from the mounting violence numbered into the hundreds. Bastiat was in the streets frequently and spent his time giving medical aid to the wounded, whatever their role in the revolution. The results of one "massacre" of 52 revolutionaries in an earlier confrontation with the Guard were not long in coming. Someone located a wagon on which all the corpses could be placed. A man stood on top of the pile, holding a torch aloft for the people of Paris

to see the crime that had been committed. The torch lighted
the body of a young woman on top of the pile of bodies with
her bloody breast bared. All night long the funeral wagon
went from place to place throughout Paris. The great crowd
following the wagon went to the doors of home after home,
waking people and forcing them out into the street to view the
bodies. Outside Paris, railways and bridges had been destroyed
in all directions for a distance of some thirty miles. Food and
other critical supplies—except wine which flowed freely—
were all but stopped from entering the city. Frightened citizens cringed in their homes, crowds of ruffians stepped over
the dead bodies still lying in the streets to demand that all
houses acknowledge the new republic by means of colored
devices or lamps placed in the windows. Those houses without
them were attacked.

"The Democratic Disease of Envy"

Surveying the wreckage of the Revolution of 1848, Tocqueville wrote that one of the causes was:

> . . . the democratic disease of envy, that was silently permeating
> it; the economic and political theories that were beginning to make
> their way and that strove to prove that human misery was the work
> of laws and not of Providence, and that poverty could be suppressed
> by changing the conditions of society; the contempt into which the
> governing class, and especially the men who led it, had fallen, a
> contempt so general and so profound that it paralysed the resistance
> even of those who were most interested in maintaining the power
> that was being overthrown; the centralization that reduced the
> whole revolutionary movement to the over-master of Paris and the
> seizing of the machinery of government; and lastly, the mobility
> of all this, institutions, ideas, men, customs, in a fluctuating state
> of society that had, in less than sixty years, undergone the shock

of seven great revolutions, without numbering a multitude of smaller, secondary upheavals.

Bastiat's own judgment on the Revolution of 1848 was that it was no victory at all, but another attack on individual freedom, for it was contemptuous of law and order as well as the free market. Its leaders were just as indecisive and ineffectual as those of the members of the old Chamber of Deputies. Without Louis Philippe, the public no longer had a convenient scapegoat on which to blame all the ills that still persisted and it was angrier than ever.

Events in Paris triggered other uprisings throughout Europe. German university students and Hungarian and Italian peasants took to the streets and revolution spread. Bastiat had warned as much, but he took no comfort in seeing his prophecies fulfilled.

CHAPTER 5

The Triumph of French Democracy

> ... you cannot legislate fraternity without legislating injustice.

THE 1840s IN FRANCE HAD SPAWNED A HOST OF enemies for the *bourgeois* monarchy. Many men had seen the approaching revolutionary possibilities in France and were carefully preparing for their own role in the government that they felt would follow Louis Philippe. As is usually the case, they found it far easier to agree that the old structure should be deposed than to agree upon what new structure should be erected in its place.

The self-styled provisional government that had been meeting at the Hotel de Ville soon demonstrated, in fact, that its members could agree on little else besides their common animosity to Louis Philippe. Several of the members even maintained spies to keep tabs on their colleagues. One French wit, viewing the membership of the provisional government and their constant posturings and maneuvers against one another, commented that it was "as if Providence had deliberately thrown together all varieties of human pride, in order to show how little this sentiment could accomplish."

Under Lamartine and Blanc, the work of the provisional government staggered forward, but from the beginning the two men were at personal as well as political loggerheads. And the entire situation was badly complicated by the continuing revolutionary unrest in the streets of Paris. Members of the Parisian mob were quite willing to walk into meetings of the provisional government and announce their demands. The clear threat of further violence hung in the air. The streets were still barricaded and the socialists and communists were threatening to overthrow the provisional government in just the same way that the members of the provisional government had overthrown the monarchy. Lamartine, one of the nation's most popular poets and orators, tried again and again to pacify the mob. Once, in desperation, he shouted to those gathered outside the Hotel de Ville, "What do you want?" One member of the crowd shouted back, "Your head!" That ended the discussion for Lamartine, who retired inside the hotel to attend further deliberations of the provisional government. Though a regime was finally established under Lamartine, he and his fellow members in the government never recovered from the enormous surprise of finding themselves in charge of the French state. They simply weren't prepared to govern or to face down the socialists and communists who demanded "an equal division of property" and "Bread or Blood!"

Agitators were willing to keep the people stirred up as a means of embarrassing the new government. It was during this period that a thousand plans of every conceivable description were put forth for the salvation of the French people. All these plans had in common the use of great centralized control to achieve social objectives. They appeared in the newspapers, on street corner placards and in the mouths of soap-box orators wherever a crowd would gather. All inequalities of fortune, education, property, and even sex were to be done away with. Poverty was to be specifically outlawed. Work was to become a thing of the past. It was in such an environment that the new government assumed power.

Under increasing pressure to proclaim a republic, the provisional government finally acquiesced when the crowd broke into its meetings and unfurled a huge banner on which, written in charcoal, appeared the slogan, "The Republic One and Indivisible Is Declared." Concluding a hard night of drafting decrees and distributing portfolios, the weary members of the provisional government greeted the dawn with a breakfast of black bread and cheese, washed down with red wine drunk from a cracked sugar bowl that was passed from man to man around the room. Lamartine murmured, "a good beginning for economy in government." Thus, the Second French Republic came into existence.

The first nation to recognize the new French state was the United States of America. The American minister in Paris, Richard Rush, took it upon himself to applaud publicly the triumph of democracy that he felt he had just witnessed. Soon other diplomatic recognitions were extended to the Second French Republic. Even Frenchmen began to believe that such an entity actually existed. Just as Frenchmen of the 1789 vintage had called one another "citizen," and revolutionary Russians of a later date would call one another "comrade," the 1848 revolutionaries referred to one another as "laborer." "Trees of Liberty" were soon planted throughout Paris and decorated with a variety of flags and ribbons commemorating the new regime. Along the Champs Elysées, young boys took shots at a clay image of Louis Philippe. For those who hit the statue in the eye, the prize was a miniature statue of liberty. Enthusiasm and good feeling ran high among nearly all sections of the population. Rumors were circulating that under the new republic a "laborer" would be able to live for nothing, and no one would ever need pay rent again. Some of the property owners who refused to cooperate in this grand new scheme soon found their buildings decorated with black flags and surrounded by straw piles that appeared suspiciously convenient in case arson was later decided upon.

The first problem of the new government centered upon a socialist demand that the red flag should be used to replace the French tricolor. Soon a mob had gathered at the Hotel de Ville to demand that the provisional government adopt a new flag. A hasty conference with the financial advisers of the new regime made it clear that the red flag would ruin all hope of international credit for the new government. That settled it for Lamartine, who went out and faced the mob, whose muskets were leveled at him while he spoke. The drama of the situation caused the spell-binder to rise to even greater heights than usual, and he managed to produce a powerful surge of patriotism in the crowd, reminding them that the tricolor had gone round the world in triumph. Thus passed the first days of government by mob.

Priscilla Robertson's *Revolutions of 1848* contains a fascinating sketch of the man called upon to lead the new "government by mob":

Lamartine was born an aristocrat, with more ties to the Bourbon than to the Orleans dynasty. In 1830 he seemed too conservative for the new government of Louis Philippe, and people expected that he would retire and write more of the lyrics that made him one of France's leading poets. But Lamartine wanted to be a statesman and in 1833 won election to the Chamber. When people asked him whether he would sit on the right or the left, he laughingly answered "on the ceiling," for his design was to keep away from party intrigues for a period, well out of trouble, while he polished up his public speaking. In order to learn how to make his words purple and golden (as Louis Blanc assures us they were in 1848), he practiced on social and humanitarian subjects rather than on political ones. It is no wonder that his colleagues did not know what to make of him, or that when he formally entered the left in 1843 its members were alarmed.

To Tocqueville, the head of the Second French Republic was an absolutely unprincipled politician: "I do not know that I have ever . . . met a mind so void of any thought of the public welfare as his . . . . Neither have I ever known a mind less sincere . . . . When speaking or writing he spoke the truth or lied, without caring which he did, occupied only with the effect he wished to produce at the moment." The common rumor of the time was that Lamartine had pledged his support to the government of Louis Philippe in last-minute secret sessions when it appeared that the government might remain standing but had changed sides and immediately came out in favor of outright revolution because the prospect of becoming president of the new republic seemed the only means of staving off his creditors.

Lamartine had already been a major political figure and a member of the Chamber of Deputies long before the February Revolution. He and Bastiat had been in correspondence for some three years prior. He had publicly advanced the thesis that government had an obligation to supply jobs to all those able and willing to work. Bastiat had immediately challenged that assumption, and Lamartine had written to him privately, admitting the truth of Bastiat's analysis. Lamartine professed himself to be so impressed with Bastiat's ideas that he spoke from the same platform as the young man during an 1846 meeting in Marseilles, endorsing free trade in general and the work of Frederic Bastiat in particular.

The friendly association of the two men continued until the eve of the revolution. In fact, Lamartine had written to Bastiat shortly before, "If ever the storm carries me to Power, you will help me carry out our ideas." Bastiat was apparently offered a high position in the new regime, but preferred to retain his freedom of criticism. And criticize he did. When Lamartine began to make speeches referring to the necessity for fraternity as enforced by government in various social welfare measures, Bastiat directly protested:

> Only justice can be demanded from the law, which acts by means of coercion. He [Lamartine] thought that people can, in addition, expect fraternity from the law. Last August he wrote me: "If ever, in a time of crisis, I find myself placed at the helm, your idea will be half of my creed."
>
> And I reply to him here: "The second half of your creed will stifle the first, for you cannot legislate fraternity without legislating injustice."
>
> When, under the pretext of fraternity, the legal code imposes mutual sacrifices on the citizens, human nature is not thereby abrogated. Everyone will then direct his efforts toward contributing little to, and taking much from, the common fund of sacrifices. Now, is it the most unfortunate who gain in this struggle? Certainly not, but rather the most influential and calculating.

Such frankness was not calculated to make Bastiat a favorite. The appointments of the new regime were no more attractive than the regime itself. The novelist George Sand was given a position writing propaganda in the ministry of the interior. A life-long socialist devotee and enthusiast for every left-wing cause, George Sand's first reaction was, "I have seen the people, grand, sublime, generous, the most admirable people in the universe." After a few months' experience in the regime, she wrote, "The majority of the French people are blind, credulous, ignorant, ungrateful, bad and stupid. . . ."

The portfolio of finance was entrusted to a well-to-do Parisian banker. He took one look at the financial position of the new government and vowed that he would rather commit suicide than share responsibility for the government. Lamartine looked about for a replacement financier and discovered him in Louis Antoine Garnier-Pages, who promptly restored credit by declaring the notes of the Bank of France to be legal tender, not redeemable in specie. This in effect relieved the new regime of all its financial responsibilities, so long as it could force its worthless notes upon its legions of creditors.

Labor arbitration for the Second Republic was assigned to the Paris chief of police. Soon his office was running a free employment agency and had taken over the placement of all Parisian workers. He "solved" labor-management relations by forbidding all strikes by police order. One of the especially effective means of handling the unemployed was to recruit them as members of the National Guard, or the *Gardes Mobiles*. Soon there were some 90,000 new members in Paris alone. Neither the social role nor the coercive power of the state seemed to be shrinking under the new government.

Bastiat Comes to the Assembly

The radical turmoil of Paris under the new regime did much to alienate the French provinces. Elections for the new constituent assembly under the Second Republic were pending, and the provinces were determined to curb the radicalism of the Lamartine regime by the election of a more moderate assembly. For years Paris had ruled France, neither wisely nor well, and the provinces were determined not to allow a socialist takeover.

Frederic Bastiat was similarly determined to fight socialism. Events in Paris demanded that he make every effort to stand as a spokesman. He returned to his district in Landes to campaign for the legislature. Soon he had founded a journal, *La république Française,* in an effort to bring his ideas before the general public. In it, he asked the question, "Now that we have torn down, must we not begin to build anew?" That "building anew" could only begin, he felt, when France truly had "protection for all rights, those of the conscience as well as those of intelligence; those of property, like those of work; those of the family as those of the commune; those of the country as those of humanity."

Bastiat met with success and was soon elected as a deputy to the new National Assembly. As the date approached for him to leave his beloved Mugron and return to the bitter debates and pressing problems that he knew would face him in Paris, he took stock of himself and his life. He had in his mind the idea for one brilliant all-encompassing study that would serve as his statement of the proper social order. And he was desperately afraid that the life which he faced in Paris would prevent his completion of his idea. His tuberculosis had now advanced to the point that he realized his mission in Paris might be a virtual sentence of death.

Arriving in Paris, Bastiat found in the capital one hundred thousand armed workmen, dying of hunger, but filled to the brim with the wild theories and visionary hopes implanted in them by demagogues. Another returning legislator described the scene:

I saw society cut into two; those who possessed nothing, united in a common greed; those who possessed something, united in a common terror. There were no bonds, no sympathy between these two great sections; everywhere the idea of an inevitable and immediate struggle seemed at hand. Already the bourgeois and the people . . . had come to blows, with varying fortunes, at Rouen, Limoges, Paris; not a day passed but the owners of property were attacked or menaced in either their capital or income: they were asked to employ labor without selling the produce; they were expected to remit the rents of their tenants when they themselves possessed no other means of living.

At last the National Assembly met on May 4, though it was far from clear until the last moment whether the group would meet at all. The mob was demanding that the government remove all guarantees of property, substituting guarantees of a livelihood for all Frenchmen and for the satisfaction of every "need." Bastiat himself had expected a difficult situation in the new Assembly, but the reality was even worse. Fifteen times during the first sitting the members competed with one another in shouting, "Long live the Republic!" This was probably less from Republican enthusiasm than from a desire on the part of most of the individual members to demonstrate their alleged enthusiasm for egalitarian causes. An early decree of the provisional government had demanded that the representatives in the French Assembly should wear an extravagant revolutionary uniform, though few members actually adopted that style of dress. The Assembly was a bedlam, filled with political hatred and jealousy and yet bound by fear of the Parisian mob.

In an attempt to imitate the National Convention which had convened following the Revolution of 1789, the men with the most radical and most revolutionary opinions immediately adopted the custom of sitting on the highest benches within the Assembly chamber. Calling themselves the Montagnards, those on the highest benches were a mixture of old-school revolutionaries and new school socialists. The men like Bastiat and Tocqueville were a slender minority.

The Struggle Begins

Lamartine was now at the height of his popularity. He had not only been elected to the National Assembly by the city of Paris, but had also been elected by eleven other departments throughout France. All parties looked to him as a savior. The socialists regarded him as a man on the left. The anti-socialists regarded him as the only possible leader who attracted wide enough support to stop the socialist tide. This attitude of the anti-socialists is very difficult to understand, considering the major role which Lamartine had played in the February Revolution. It can be explained only by the fact that the National Assembly was so badly frightened by the revolutionary Paris with which it found itself surrounded, was so blinded by its terror of the people, that it temporarily forgot Lamartine's involvement in the same revolutionary activities. Perhaps Lamartine looked so much less frightening than the other revolutionary leaders that the anti-socialists forgot to be frightened of him at all.

Whatever the reason for his power, Lamartine began to make immediate use of it, generally for socialist purposes of which Bastiat heartily disapproved. While poor health prevented him from strong speaking performances, Bastiat nevertheless sometimes addressed the Assembly. On other occasions, he wrote out speeches in a style in which they would have been delivered and then published them in various pamphlets and in Paris newspapers. As the result, Bastiat and his words were very much on the scene during the Lamartine regime and were invariably in bitter opposition to the direction Lamartine was taking. Some of the lectures that Bastiat delivered to the socialists in these days must have taken great personal courage. They also reflected the intellect and principled position of a man who saw far more clearly than most the direction his country was taking.

Lamartine had proposed a national exposition, to be financed in Paris by government funds. He had pointed out how the expenditure of these government funds would be a tremendous boost to employment, painting a moving picture of all the painters, masons, decorators, costumers, architects, and other workmen who would thus find their position improved and who would then be able to provide necessities for themselves and for their children. Lamartine concluded his speech to the Assembly amidst cheers and approval, insisting: "It is to them that you give these 60,000 francs."

To the Assembly's cries of "Very good!" Bastiat replied, "Very bad!":

> Yes, it is, at least in part, to the workers in the theaters that the sixty thousand francs in question will go. A few scraps might well get lost on the way. If one scrutinized the matter closely, one might even discover that most of the pie will find its way elsewhere. The workers will be fortunate if there are a few crumbs left for them! But I should like to assume that the entire subsidy will go to the painters, decorators, costumers, hairdressers, etc. That is what is *seen*.
>
> But where does it come from? This is the other side of the coin, just as important to examine as its face. What is the source of these

sixty thousand francs? And where would they have gone if a legislative vote had not first directed them to the Rue de Rivoli and from there to the Rue de Grenelle [from the City Hall to the theatrical suppliers on the Left Bank]? That is what is *not seen*.

Surely, no one will dare maintain that the legislative vote has caused this sum to hatch out from the ballot box; that it is a pure addition to the national wealth; that, without this miraculous vote, these 60,000 francs would have remained invisible and impalpable. It must be admitted that all that the majority can do is to decide that they will be taken from somewhere to be sent somewhere else, and that they will have one destination only by being deflected from another.

This being the case, it is clear that the taxpayer who will have been taxed one franc will no longer have this franc at his disposal. It is clear that he will be deprived of a satisfaction to the tune of one franc, and that the worker, whoever he is, who would have procured this satisfaction for him, will be deprived of wages in the same amount.

Let us not, then, yield to the childish illusion of believing that the vote of May 16 adds anything whatever to national well-being and employment. It reallocates possessions, it reallocates wages, and that is all. . . . When it is a question of taxes, gentlemen, prove their usefulness by reason with some foundation, but not with that lamentable assertion: "Public spending keeps the working class alive." It makes the mistake of covering up a fact that it is essential to know: namely, that public spending is always a substitute for private spending and that consequently it may well support one worker in place of another but adds nothing to the lot of the working class taken as a whole. Your argument is fashionable, but it is quite absurd, for the reasoning is not correct.

Bastiat returned to the attack again and again as similar measures were debated before the Assembly. Socialist orators proposed universal credit, underwritten by government funds. They proposed the development of the Algerian colony, including large scale subsidies for its propagation, and even the relocation of a substantial number of Frenchmen. In item after item, ranging from government aid to the needy to the most elaborate plans for government control of the economy, the socialists, spurred on by pressures from the Parisian population, brought up measures that Bastiat analyzed and attacked. As he wrote at the time:

> Four orators are all trying to be heard in the Assembly. At first they speak all at once, then one after the other. What have they said? Very beautiful things, surely, about the power and grandeur of France, the necessity of sowing in order to reap. . . . The modern socialist factions ceaselessly oppose free association in present-day society. They do not realize that a free society is a true association much superior to any of those that they concoct out of their fertile imaginations.
>
> The socialists who have invented these follies, and who in days of distress plant them in the minds of the masses, generously confer on themselves the title of "forward-looking" men, and there is a real danger that usage, that tyrant of language, will ratify both the word and the judgment it implies. "Forward-looking" assumes that these gentlemen can see ahead much further than ordinary people; that their only fault is to be too much in advance of their century; and that, if the time is not yet arrived when certain private services, allegedly parasitical, can be eliminated, the fault is with the public, which is far behind socialism. To *my* mind and knowledge, it is the contrary that is true, and I do not know to what barbaric century we should have to return to find on this point a level of understanding comparable to the socialists.
>
> The more one examines these "forward-looking" schools of thought, the more one is convinced that at bottom they rest on nothing but ignorance proclaiming itself infallible and demanding despotic power in the name of this infallibility.

National Workshops

Bastiat's constant exposure of the failures and distortions of the left did little to stop them. Under Louis Blanc's chairmanship, the Luxembourg Commission drew up a report advocating near-total socialism. A series of communes were to be set up, supplemented by a full system of social security. Socialists were also determined that the state must provide full employment for all Frenchmen. Blanc had already made "the right to employment" a major issue in previous years.

The National Workshops were a major feature of the system that was finally adopted by the Assembly. Members were given an insignia, a golden bee, to wear on their caps. The officers wore woolen armbands. Soon golden bees appeared everywhere in Paris, with the clear implication in the minds of many that the National Workshops marked the eventual end of not only private employment but private property. Bastiat warned:

> A new right clamors for entry into the Constitution: *the right to employment*. It does not merely ask for a place of its own; it lays claim wholly or partly to the place now held by *the right to property*.
> M. Louis Blanc has already provisionally claimed this new right and we know with what success.
> M. Proudon demands it in order to abolish property rights entirely . . . Thus, according to these political theorists, there is in property something unjust and false, a deadly germ. I propose to demonstrate that property is truth and justice itself and that what it has within is the principle of progress and life.

Most Frenchmen outside Paris hated the National Workshops and the man they felt primarily responsible for them, Louis Blanc. They had also begun to distrust Lamartine because he seemed unable to face down the socialists. In particular, the hopes of property-conscious Frenchmen centered on the newly elected Assembly. Could the Assembly stop the mobs and the socialists? The question of force was also in the air. No one knew where the loyalty of the National Guard would lie in a crisis.

In May of 1848, the next crisis moved closer, day by day. More and more people roamed the streets of Paris. The galleries and even the floor of the Assembly was always jammed. Enrollment in the National Workshops exceeded 100,000, then 120,000, with no end in sight. The question of what to do with this exploding state entity became so emotionally charged that it was never broached in the Assembly out of fear of a negative public reaction.

Instead, the members spent the month of May assuring the people of France that all "unnecessary and unpopular" taxes would be removed. At the same time, Parisians were demanding steadily larger sums from the public purse for all sorts of schemes. Bastiat could stand no more. He wrote:

> The public has been deluged, with an unlimited prodigality, by two sorts of promises. According to one, a vast number of charitable, but costly institutions are to be established at public expense. According to the other, all taxes are going to be reduced. Thus, on the one hand, nurseries, asylums, free primary and secondary schools, workshops, and industrial retirement pensions are going to be multiplied. . . . The state is going to found credit institutions, lend to workers the tools of production, double the size of the army, reorganize the navy, etc., etc., and, on the other hand, it will abolish the tax on salt, tolls, and all the most unpopular excises.
>
> Read the last "Manifesto" of the Montagnards that they issued in connection with the presidential election. It is rather long, but can be summed up in a few words: *The state should give a great deal to the citizens and take little from them.* It is always the same tactic, or, if you will, the same error. . . . "Give nothing to the state, and receive a great deal from it."

The Approaching Clash

At the May 15 meeting of the Assembly, the streets outside its chamber were more quiet than it had been since well before the revolution. The silence was misleading: the members soon learned that they were surrounded by more than 20,000 men when the crowd at last revealed its approach with a single terrible shout. The stunned legislators kept their seats. The speaker who held the floor continued his remarks until interrupted by a member who had gone to the door and returned, announcing, ". . . General Courtais has ordered the *Gardes Mobiles* guarding the doors of the Assembly to sheath their bayonets." Immediately afterward, people began to pour through every door, surrounding the members with a mass of humanity. Some of the intruders were armed. Some were aggressive, others only astonished at having forced the legislature without resistance. All were in a state of feverish excitement. The day outside was sweltering, and the rising temperature in the over-crowded space made the chamber an unbearable place. Revolutionary slogans were muttered again and again. One man pointed to an Assembly member, "See that vulture down there? I should like to twist its neck." Tocqueville recorded what happened next:

> It was then that I saw appear . . . in the tribune a man whom I have never seen since, but the recollection of whom has always filled me with horror and disgust. He had wan, emaciated cheeks, white lips, and a sickly, wicked, repulsive expression, a dirty pallor, the appearance of a mouldy corpse; he wore no visible linen; an old black frock coat tightly covered his lean, withered limbs; he seemed to have passed his life in a sewer and to have just left it. I was told it was Blanqui.

The revolutionary leader mounted to a commanding position where he addressed the Assembly, demanding that its members should pay for the wrongs it had committed against the people. All day long, the Assembly remained in session, waiting for assistance to arrive, but there seemed to be no other souls alive in Paris. Tocqueville continued:

> This passive resistance irritated and incensed the people; it was like a cold, even surface upon which its fury glided without knowing what to catch hold of; it struggled and writhed in vain, without finding any issue to its undertaking. A thousand diverse and contradictory clamors filled the air: "Let us go away," cried some. . . . "The organization of labor . . . . A tax on the rich. . . . We want Louis Blanc!" cried others; they ended by fighting at the foot of the tribune to decide who should mount it; five or six orators occupied it at once and often all spoke together. As always happens in insurrections, the terrible was mingled with the ridiculous. The heat was so stifling that many of the first intruders left the chamber; they were forthwith replaced by others who had been waiting at the doors to come in. In this way I saw a fireman in uniform making his way down the gangway that passed along my bench. "We can't make them vote!" they shouted to him. "Wait, wait," he replied, "I'll see to it, I'll give them a piece of my mind." Thereupon he pulled his helmet over his eyes with a determined air, fastened the snap, squeezed through the crowd, pushing aside all those who stood in his way, and mounted the tribune. He imagined he would be as much at his ease there as upon a roof, but he could not find his words and stopped short. The people cried, "Speak up, fireman!" but he did not speak a word, and they ended by turning him out of the tribune. Just then a number of men of the people caught Louis Blanc in their arms and carried him in triumph round the chamber. They held him by his little legs above their heads; I saw him make vain efforts to extricate himself: he twisted and turned on every side without succeeding in escaping from their hands, talking all the while in a choking, strident voice.

He reminded me of a snake having its tail pinched. They put him down on a bench beneath mine. I heard him cry, "My friends, you have just won. . . . " but the remainder of his words were lost in the din.

At last the leaderless crowd dispersed, and a new group began to gather in the street. From that day forward, Assembly members invariably carried a brace of pistols beneath their coats. Another popular weapon was a ball of lead sewn into a short leather thong which was then fastened to the arm, a sort of portable club. The streets of Paris became as unsafe as at any moment during the earlier February Revolution. Indeed, revolution seemed on the verge of erupting again.

The incident that finally crystallized a total breakdown of order was the announcement that the National Workshops were to be disbanded. Costs had risen to such enormous heights that the Assembly could no longer guarantee payments. The leaderless mob gave into mass violence as the summer of 1848 began. France was in the throes of its second revolution within four months.

Bastiat knew the reasons why, though few would listen:

> . . . while the French people have been in advance of all other nations in the conquest of their rights, or rather of their political guarantees, they have nonetheless remained the most governed, regimented, administered, imposed upon, shackled, and exploited of all.
>
> France is also, and necessarily, the one nation in which revolutions are most likely to occur.
>
> And what remedy is proposed? To enlarge the domain of the law indefinitely, that is, the responsibility of government.
>
> But if the government undertakes to raise and regulate wages, and cannot do so; if it undertakes to assist all the unfortunate, and cannot do so; if it undertakes to assure pensions to all workers, and cannot do so; if it undertakes to provide workers with the tools of

production; and cannot do so; if it undertakes to make interest-free credit available to all those clamoring for loans and cannot do so; if in words that we regret to note were written by M. de Lamartine, "the state assumes the task of enlightening, developing, increasing, spiritualizing, and sanctifying the soul of the people," and if it fails; is it not evident that after each disappointment (alas only too probable!), there will be no less inevitable revolution?

Once we start from this idea, accepted by all our political theorists, and so energetically expressed by M. Louis Blanc in these words: "The motive force of society is the government"; once men consider themselves as sentient, but passive, capable of improving themselves morally or materially by their own intelligence and energy, and reduced to expecting everything from law; in a word, when they admit that there relation to the state is that of a flock of sheep to the shepherd, it is clear that the responsibility of government is immense. Good and evil, virtue and vice, equality and inequality, wealth and poverty, all proceed from it. It is entrusted with everything, it undertakes everything, it does everything; hence, it is responsible for everything. If we are happy, it has every right to claim our gratitude; but if we are wretched, it alone is to blame. . . .

Thus there is not a single ill afflicting the nation for which the government has not voluntarily made itself responsible. Is it astonishing, then, that each little twinge should be a cause of revolution?

CHAPTER 6

Revolution: June 1848

> Do what you will, gentlemen; you cannot give money
> to some without taking it away from others. If you abso-
> lutely insist on draining the taxpayer dry, well and good;
> but at least do not treat him like a fool. Do not tell him:
> "I am taking this money from you to repay you for what
> I have already taken from you."

TIME WAS RUNNING OUT FOR THE FRENCH GOV-
ernment by the early summer of 1848. The National Workshops had become a political, social and economic monstrosity
and the Assembly had vowed to disband them. But it had
already found itself faced with an enormous contingent of men,
organized in para-military fashion, who felt that the government owed them all they had been receiving and a good deal
more. Any attempt to disband the National Workshops was
sure to be greeted with revolutionary violence, yet every day
that the Assembly delayed in that inevitable step, the monster
grew more and more powerful and more and more rapacious.

At last the Assembly took the dreaded step, and the National Workshops were abolished. But the corruptions of the
dole had done their work well. The workmen refused to leave
the city, and on the 22nd of June they marched through the
streets in military formations, chanting endlessly, "We won't
be sent away, we won't be sent away. . . . " They then pre-
sented a series of arrogant demands to the Assembly, accom-

panied with thinly veiled threats. On June 23rd, the troops of the National Workshops (and they were troops) began building barricades. The streets of Paris were to taste blood once again.

The first strategy of Lamartine's government was to attack the barricades one by one, thus favoring a holding action rather than an all-out confrontation. But the National Guard soon found that the task they had been assigned was impossible. The situation seemed desperate, one of the Assembly members described:

> On my return I met, in the Rue des Jeuneurs, a National Guard covered with blood and fragments of brain. He was very pale and was going home. I asked him what was happening; he told me that his battalion had just received the full force of a very murderous discharge of the musketry at the Porte Saint-Denis. One of his comrades, whose name he mentioned to me, had been killed by his side, and he was covered with the blood and brains of this unhappy man.
>
> I returned to the Assembly, astonished at not having met a single soldier in the whole distance that I had traversed. It was not till I came in front of the *Palais-Bourbon* that I at last perceived great columns of infantry, marching, followed by cannon.
>
> I found the Assembly very determined, but very ill at ease; and it must be confessed there was enough to make it so. It was easy to perceive through the multitude of contradictory reports that we had to deal with the most universal, the best armed, and the most furious insurrection ever known in Paris. The National Workshops and various revolutionary bands that had just been disbanded supplied it with leaders. It was extending every moment, and it was difficult to believe that it would not end by being victorious, when one remembered that all the great insurrections of the last sixty years had triumphed. To all these enemies we were only able to oppose the battalions of the *bourgeoisie,* regiments which had been disarmed in February, and twenty thousand undisciplined lads of the *Garde Mobile,* who were all sons, brothers, or near relations of insurgents and whose dispositions were doubtful.

But what alarmed us most was our leaders. The members of the Executive Commission filled us with profound distrust. On this subject I encountered, in the Assembly, the same feeling which I had observed among the *Garde.* We doubted the good faith of some and the capacity of others. They were too numerous, besides, and too much divided to be able to act in complete harmony, and they were too much men of speech and the pen to be able to act to good purpose under such circumstances, even if they had agreed among themselves.

What saved the Assembly and saved France in its hour of crisis was the very desperation of the situation. Things were so totally out of hand and the threat was so enormous that the men of the provinces realized that the revolt had to be put down at all costs. Thousands simultaneously rose up all over France and began the journey to Paris, entering the city from every conceivable direction. Men of every class, armed in every conceivable manner; these Frenchmen knew that their country could not stand another triumph of the Parisian mobs. Tocqueville summarized the result: "It was evident from that moment that we should end by gaining the day, for the insurgents received no reinforcements, whereas we had all France for reserves."

The struggle for the control of France had been bitter indeed. Many of the houses of Paris were left in smoking ruins. Debris filled the streets. Thousands had been killed or wounded. France was continuing its horrible object lesson for the world.

Bastiat Stands Against the Tide

Though it was true that the people of France had been deeply frightened by the June uprising, much as the Romans had been frightened by the barbarian invasions, it seemed that they had learned little enough in the process. Though there was a strong reaction against the lower classes and against the Parisian mobs, there seemed no clear understanding as to the real cause of the trouble. The French population had been sufficiently frightened to be bitterly opposed to revolution, but continued to favor the socialism and government interventionism that had produced the revolution. Revolution had been put down, but the tide of socialism was still running strong.

It was Frederic Bastiat's fate to be projected into the very path of that tide and to stand almost alone against it. The events of his entire life seemed a preparation for the impossible task which now faced him. It was in this difficult and thankless undertaking that Bastiat had his finest hour, as he struggled to bring to the people of France the understanding of their own problems and institutions which they so desperately needed.

Throughout his last great crusade against socialism, Bastiat worked unceasingly, refusing to spare any attention for his rapidly failing health. Although he spoke before the Assembly only occasionally because he was having difficulty getting his breath, he turned out a flood of pamphlets and articles. In response to the socialist Louis Blanc, he wrote *Individualism and Fraternity*. In response to socialist arguments favoring abolition of private property, he wrote *Property and Law*. As issue after issue arose in the Assembly or in the popular press, Bastiat dashed off an immediate and hardhitting response. He also maintained a full-time round of duties in the Assembly itself, where he was an influential member of the Committee of Finance.

Though ill with tuberculois, Bastiat was undertaking a task beyond the powers of ten healthy men. He preferred the quiet and scholarly life, but he assumed the role of propagandist and popularizer, attempting to reach the people of France with the message of freedom at a time when the people of France demanded intervention. From the beginning, Bastiat had spoken with such complete honesty and sincerity that even many of his enemies paid close attention to his comments and ideas. As one Paris newspaper, bitterly in opposition to Bastiat's position, phrased it:

> The doctrines of the writer-economist are not our own. But we must admit that he has posed this question with all the clarity of a practical man, and that he has offered, in support of his amendment, reasons of extreme gravity, which have made a profound impression in the Assembly. Mr. Bastiat is not a good public speaker; he hesitates, he gropes around, he searches for the correct expression and doesn't always find it. But if his thoughts liberate themselves laboriously, they finish by carrying the day, armed with conclusive arguments.

Bastiat never voted with blocs. Thus, he voted sometimes with the left and sometimes with the right. In fact, the one consistent feature of Bastiat's voting record was that he always voted with the minority. Principle proved a lonely pinnacle, but the man from Mugron pursued his ideas with a deep concern for their truth, not their popularity. He demonstrated his principled stand from the first. Even at the risk of antagonizing the strongly conservative voters in his home district, he took a stand against the conviction of Louis Blanc when he was tried by the Assembly on charges of conspiracy and insurrection. Louis Blanc was not only a prominent socialist and author of the National Workshops, but was also a personal foe of Bastiat. As Bastiat explained in a letter to his friend, Coudroy: "The only thing I could do was to examine the evidence itself to see if M. Blanc was really guilty of the fact of conspiracy and insurrection. I do not believe that he was, and no one who reads his defense of his actions can believe him guilty either."

The Workers and the Demagogues

The ailing Bastiat reserved a special quality of invective, however, for the demagogues who made such impossible promises to the workers of France:

> An atheist was railing against religion, against priests, and against God. "If you keep on like this," said one of his listeners, who was not very orthodox himself, "you are going to make a pious man of me."
>
> Similarly when I hear our callow scribblers, our novelists, our reformers, our perfumed, mincing pamphleteers, gorged with ices and champagne, stuffing their portfolios with gilt-edged securities, or getting richly paid for their tirades against the egoism and individualism of our age; when I hear them disclaiming against the harshness of our institutions and bewailing the lot of wage earners and proletarians; when I see them raising to the heavens eyes full of tears at the sight of the poverty of the toiling masses—a poverty with which they never have any contact except to paint lucrative pictures of it; I am tempted to tell them: "If you go on like this, you are going to make me indifferent to the fate of the workers."

Bastiat went on to point out that the lust for political power that the demagogues engendered in the workers was the greatest possible disservice to them. Thus he described the dominant mood of France, "Hurrah for charity! Long live humanitarianism! Tomorrow we shall take the City Hall by storm." He also defended the classical economic position as set forth by Thomas Malthus, pointing out that the English economist had far more in mind than the constantly quoted passage in which he had discussed the arithmetic and geometric quantities of the food supply and the population. Bastiat understood that Malthus was entirely mistaken about the ultimate prospects for starvation of the human race, and yet had great merit as a proponent of classical economic principles. Once Bastiat publicly challenged Pierre Leroux, a French philosopher and editor of *Le Globe* after Leroux had written a chapter against Malthus. Bastiat began by quoting some of the opinions expressed in Malthus' "Essay on Population," and realized, as he pursued the point, that Leroux did not actually know the work of Malthus. Never one to do things by halves, Bastiat asked, "You have refuted Malthus, but have you by any chance read him through from one end to the other?"

"I have not read him at all," Leroux replied. "His whole system is set forth on one page and can be summed up in his famous arithmetical and geometrical rations. That's enough for me."

"Apparently," Bastiat said, "you care nothing for the public, for Malthus, for the truth, for conscience, or for yourself." That night, he wrote: "This is the way an opinion gains acceptance in France. Fifty ignoramuses repeat in chorus some absurd libel that has been thought up by an even bigger ignoramus; and, if only it happens to coincide to some slight degree with prevailing attitudes and passions, it becomes a self-evident truth."

The inherent contradictions in the posturings of the left were apparent to Bastiat. For example, he noted that the extreme left was "the natural enemy of all imaginable governments," yet at the same time advocated "absorption by the government of all rights and all functions." Another contradiction which Bastiat delighted in pointing out again and again was the fundamental fallacy in the assumption that government could do something for the people that the people would somehow not be expected to pay for to the last penny. Relief for the taxpayer was perpetually promised, yet seemed long delayed:

>   A few days ago, people expected to see the mechanism of representative government create an utterly novel product that its wheels had not yet succeeded in grinding out: the relief of the taxpayer.
>   Everyone anxiously awaited the outcome; the experiment affected men's pocketbooks as much as it aroused their curiosity. No one, then, doubted that the machine had sufficient impulsion, because when self-interest and novelty turn the wheels, it runs admirably at all times, in all places, during all seasons, and under all circumstances.
>   But as for reforms tending to simplify and equalize the costs of government and to render them less burdensome, no one yet knows what it can do.
>   People said: "You will soon see. Now is the time. This is a job for the fourth session, when public approval is worth something. [Bastiat here refers to the meetings of the Assembly held in every fourth year, prior to elections, describing a practice well developed in our own political life.] In 1842, we got the railroads; in 1846, we are to get a lowering of the salt tax and postal rates; we shall have to wait until 1850 for the reform of the tariff and a change in our system of indirect taxation. The fourth session is the jubilee year for the taxpayer."

Bastiat, of course, knew what most taxpayers still had to learn—government cannot devise means for giving back more than it has taken: "Do what you will, gentlemen; you cannot give money to some without taking it away from others. If you absolutely insist on draining the taxpayer dry, well and good; but at least do not treat him like a fool. Do not tell him: 'I am taking this money from you to repay you for what I have already taken from you.' "

Communism

The new government made a great point of insisting that its policies were designed to stop communism. This appeal to the fears of the French people was fostered especially by one of the key ministers in the new government, Thiers. As Bastiat well knew, Thiers had been a powerful friend of government intervention, especially in the area of tariffs. Yet this same Thiers was now posing as a leader in the struggle against communism. As Bastiat caustically commented:

> There is good reason to say that the ways of God are as infallible as they are inscrutable. For if you will just grant me for a moment that protectionism, when it becomes widespread, becomes communism, just as a little carp becomes a big carp, provided that God lets it live, I shall show you how odd it is that a champion of protectionism should pose as the destroyer of communism; but what is still more extraordinary and still more reassuring is that a powerful organization that was formed to disseminate the theory and practice of communism (in so far as this is deemed profitable to its members) should today devote half of its resources to destroying the evil it has done with the other half.
>
> This is, I repeat, a reassuring spectacle. It reassures us as to the inevitable triumph of truth, since it shows us the first authentic disseminations of subversive doctrines, frightened by their success, now concocting the antidote and the poison in the same laboratory.

Bastiat pointed out in January 1849 that the *Moniteur industriel,* a publication designed to press for government intervention in favor of business, especially as regarded tariffs, was urging a similar extortion of other people's property that the same men were quick to decry when it was applied to their own property. He clearly described the strange self-delusion that blinds men from seeing the truth about themselves and their ideas:

> What likelihood is there that the great manufacturers, respectable landowners, rich bankers, and able statesmen have made of themselves, without knowing or desiring it, the initiators and the apostles of communism in France? . . . There are many workers full of a sincere faith in the right to employment, and consequently communists without knowing or desiring it, who would not tolerate their being considered as such. The reason for this is that in all classes of society, self-interest influences the will; and the will, as Pascal says, is the principal organ of belief. Many industrialists, otherwise quite respectable, promote communism (under another name), as people always do, that is, on condition that only the goods of others are to be divided and shared. But as soon as the principle has gained ground, and it is now a matter of sharing their own property too, oh, then communism strikes them with horror. Previously, they circulated the *Moniteur industriel;* now they are distributing the book on property. To be astonished at this, one must be ignorant of the human heart, its inner springs, and its proclivity toward clever casuistry.

In a pamphlet entitled, *Protectionism and Communism,* Bastiat boldly and directly addressed Minister Thiers, demolishing point by point the entire argument for government tariffs or subsidies of any kind and demonstrating again that no difference in principle existed to separate the policies of government intervention from the policies of out-and-out communism. Both were engaged in a war on property.

The Proper Role of Government

In his continuing struggle against socialism, Bastiat warned that the present temper of the French people to expect the government to be the solution of all their problems would not only fail to solve the problems, but would generate a bureaucracy penalizing material prosperity as well as freedom. In one speech before the National Assembly, he won the applause of his fellow members with a statement against such bureaucracy:

> I am a firm believer in the ideas of Malthus when it comes to bureaucrats. For their expansion in numbers and projects is fixed precisely by Malthus' principle that the size of the population is determined by the amount of available food. If we vote 800 million francs for government services, the bureaucrats will devour 800 million; if we give them two billion, they will immediately expand themselves and their projects up to the full amount.

Building on his insistence that all government intervention amounted to a war on property and therefore to communism, Bastiat attempted to contrast a proper social framework with the government-controlled framework of his time:

> We recognize the right of every man to perform services for himself or to serve others according to conditions arrived at through free bargaining. Communism denies this right, since it places all services in the hands of an arbitrary, central authority.
>
> Our doctrine is based on private property. Communism is based on systematic plunder, since it consists in handing over to one man, without compensation, the labor of another. If it distributed to each one according to his labor, it would, in fact, recognize private property and would no longer be communism.
>
> Our doctrine is based on liberty. In fact, private property and

liberty, in our eyes are one and the same; for man is made the owner of his own services by his right and his ability to dispose of them as he sees fit. Communism destroys liberty, for it permits no one to dispose freely of his own labor.

In his most famous book, *The Law,* Bastiat described socialism and communism, under whatever labels they might appear, as forms of legalized plunder. Recognizing that the law is organized force, Bastiat made it clear that such legal plunder could only be organized injustice. He went on to emphasize that such organized injustice finally proves so corrupting to the fabric of society as to destroy all social progress and, ultimately, all individual development.

For the planner devoted to government intervention in the lives of men, such interference with personal development seems a small price to pay, since, "All of them look upon the relations between mankind and the legislator as the same as those which exist between the clay and the potter."

Disarmament

As a classical 19th-century liberal, Bastiat saw the close connection between tariffs and war. Thus, there developed in him the insistent impression that one of the primary means of maintaining great and steadily expanding power over the lives of its citizens was the capacity of the government to generate an atmosphere of crisis. One hundred years before conservatives in America discovered what was being done to their society, Bastiat had already grasped the essence of what we would later call "perpetual war for perpetual peace." He therefore included French military adventures in the catalogue of government foibles that he attacked.

Insisting that there was a fundamental conflict between vast military expenditures and prosperity at home, Bastiat caustically dismissed the idea that government spending somehow produced prosperity. He insisted that money spent for some public purpose was at best only money which would have otherwise been spent for a private purpose, perhaps of more lasting value than cartridges, uniforms, military salaries, and troop ships. Speaking before the Assembly, Bastiat once suggested that the French army was totally out of proportion to the nation's needs. One member of the Assembly rose to his feet and shouted to Bastiat, "But in June [during the June Revolution] you were not sorry to have the army!"

Bastiat responded, "You reproach me with the month of June. But I say that if we had not had such excessive armies, we would not have had the month of June." He then went on to suggest that, if there were indeed a national profit in increasing the size of the army, why would it not profit France to call the whole male population to the colors?

There is also some evidence that, during the late fall of 1849, Bastiat went to England as a secret but official delegate from the French government to discuss the possibility of arms reduction. Not much is known about that trip, but it is true that Bastiat and Cobden had earlier exchanged a considerable amount of correspondence on the possibilities involved. Certainly Bastiat saw free trade and limited government as the ideal means for attaining lasting peace and genuine freedom. In his stand against military adventurism, he was, as in so many other things, standing on principle against the dominant emotional tide of his times.

Unpopular Causes

Frederic Bastiat's penchant for unpopular causes was perhaps most clearly demonstrated in his strong public stand against the proposal to outlaw industrial unions. The National Workshops and the resultant revolutionary disturbances had so aroused the French people that the Assembly was in the process of forcing through a bill rendering illegal any form of worker organization whatsoever. On the day of the debate, the Assembly was so aroused that it was difficult for a speaker to make himself heard over the tumult. Weakened by disease and already entering the last year of his life, Bastiat rose to make this unpopular cause his own: "Citizens, I do not bring into this discussion any partisan spirit or any class prejudice. I shall not seek to play upon your emotions, but the Assembly sees that my lungs cannot struggle against parliamentary tumults; I need its kindest attention." Speaking against Articles 413, 415, and 416 of the Penal Code, Bastiat warned that the Assembly was in the process of establishing a dangerous precedent when it outlawed peaceful organization of any kind: ". . . gentlemen, an action that is innocent in itself is not criminal because it is multiplied by a certain number of men. When an action is bad in itself, I admit that if that action is performed by a certain number of individuals, one may say that it is aggravated; but when it is innocent in itself, it cannot become criminal because it is the deed of a great number of individuals."

Still speaking over the constant uproar of the Assembly, Bastiat insisted that any law which prohibited strikes would be a law enforcing slavery under another name. He pressed the point that respect for the law could only be founded upon a legal system which repressed intimidation and violence. Once the law became an institution of intimidation and violence itself, all respect for law would be at an end:

> . . . only principles have the power to satisfy men's minds, to win their hearts, and to gain the consent of their consciences. They have asked us: "Do you wish to proclaim freedom simply out of platonic love of freedom?" I, for my part, reply, "Yes." Freedom may entail trials for nations, but it alone enlightens, teaches, and edifies them. Outside of freedom, there is only oppression, and friends of order should bear in mind that this is no longer the time, if there ever was one, when the union of classes, respect for the law, security of interests, and the tranquillity of nations can be founded on oppression.
>
> In France we love freedom very much, but we hardly understand it. Oh, let us try to understand it better! We shall not love it any the less.

The Sick Republic

What Bastiat struggled against was a very old democratic disease: a willingness to deny the rights of property to others and to substitute governmental authority for individual rights. While he stood on principle, most Frenchmen rallied around plunder. In so doing, in his willingness to stand alone, he won the respect of his enemies. Even the old socialist Proudhon could write, some months before Bastiat's death, "He is devoted, body and soul, to the Republic, to liberty, equality, to progress; he has clearly proved that devotion many times with his vote in the Assembly. But in spite of that we list M. Bastiat among the men who oppose us."

Meanwhile, the voters of Landes showed their approval by returning Bastiat to the Assembly for a second term.

CHAPTER 7

Last Days

What gives me courage is . . . the thought that, perhaps,
my life may not have been useless to mankind.

TIME WAS RUNNING OUT FOR THE SECOND FRENCH
Republic and for Frederic Bastiat. Bastiat well knew that the
end was in sight, not only for his mortal efforts, but for the
sick nation which staggered on toward its rendezvous with the
man on horseback. His name: Louis Napoleon.

Even as Assembly members met to draw up the constitution
for the Second French Republic, the Republic was expiring.
The Committee for the Constitution itself gave evidence of the
sad state of affairs in France. Personally acquainted with the
members of the draft committee, Tocqueville regarded some
of them as "chimerical visionaries." One member, Victor Considérant, Tocqueville found especially discouraging for the future of the new republic: "[He] would have deserved to be
sent to a lunatic asylum had he been sincere—but I fear he
deserved more than that." Tocqueville described the other
committee members as being totally unaware of any lasting
principles or purposes, totally bewildered at the prospect of
deciding the course of action for France.

All this bore very little resemblance to the men, so certain
of their objects and so well acquainted with the measures
necessary to attain them, who 60 years before, under George

Washington's presidency, so successfully drew up the U.S. Constitution. When it was drawn up, the French version proved almost unbelievably complex, guaranteeing a deadlock between the president and the Assembly, and almost guaranteeing that a dictator would step forward to break the impasse. The would-be dictator was ready at hand. Louis Napoleon Bonaparte had twice attempted inept coups and had been stopped each time with little more than a pat on the head. He had been dismissed as an absurd character, quite incapable of harming France. Perhaps this is why, in the balloting for the first president under the new constitution, so many of the French leaders threw their support to Louis Napoleon. Surely here was a man whom the politicians could control. How mistaken they were.

The Man on Horseback: Louis Napoleon

Nonetheless, all France soon sang the praises of Louis Napoleon and fully three-quarters of the voting population cast their support to him. The years 1848 and 1849 had been filled with violent revolution, erupting first in France and then spreading to Vienna, Munich, Milan, Berlin, and Rome. The times had moved too fast and had been too frightening for many people. Perhaps a milquetoast in the presidency would give time for the tide of change to subside.

Bastiat had thrown his support to General Cavaignac as a candidate in the presidential election. Even in the face of Louis Napoleon's overwhelming popularity, Bastiat refused to give ground. He told the electors of his district how he felt and flatly announced that if they had other ideas and other hopes for France than those which he expressed, then he was not the man to represent them in office. The election of December 10,

1849, which swept Louis Napoleon into office made it clear that the people did indeed wish a change. Even then, Bastiat refused to compromise in any way. When the Assembly members visited the new president as a group to offer their good wishes, he refused to accompany the delegation.

While the people of France wished to go in a new direction, they had no idea of what direction. They had been quick to revolt against government which did not seem to do their bidding, but they showed little capacity to chart their own course. This was evident in their desperate haste to write the new constitution, as well as their rush to embrace Louis Napoleon as president. No working majority seemed to stand in favor of any principle. During the presidential election, there had been five different Napoleonic newspapers published in Paris, stressing a variety of positions ranging from the extreme left to the extreme right. Each claimed Napoleon's position as their own. Nothing could have displayed the confusion of the French people better than Napoleon's election after such a campaign. Tocqueville mused, "the world is a strange theatre. There are moments in it when the worst plays are those which succeed best. If Louis Napoleon had been a wise man, or a man of genius, he could never have become president of the Republic." In perspective, it becomes clear that the French were unable to achieve either lasting stability or a free society because they could not cope with their deeply inbred tradition of centralization. All power had been drawn into too few hands, and, while those hands constantly changed, the enormous centralization of power did not. As the result, the life of the Second French Republic was to be little longer than the time remaining to Frederic Bastiat. But at a time of such confusion and distress, the magic name of Napoleon seemed to bring with it a vision of prestige, glory and order.

The French, of all European peoples, had been most ad-
dicted to martial glory and ready to accept any privation or
disruption so long as it promised the extravagant satisfactions
of a sweeping foreign policy. Louis Napoleon, with the unerr-
ing sense of a politician, perceived that a militant and breast-
beating foreign policy, in the tradition of the first Napoleon,
would provide the issue he needed to move far beyond the
simple position of president of the Second French Republic.
He hid his thoughts behind the grey-blue, almond shaped
eyes through which he calculated the world and its occupants.
As one visitor described those striking eyes, "If they were the
windows of his soul their blinds were constantly down." He
impressed one visitor to the presidential palace as "an obvious
opium eater," because of the utter lack of personal effusion
which he displayed. With his German background, he retained a lifelong difficulty with the French language, though
his deliberate and calculated manner helped him partially to
overcome the deficiency. However poorly Louis Napoleon
spoke their language, he understood the French citizens' psychological need for martial glory, and promptly commenced a
series of interventions in Roman, Polish and Hungarian political affairs. Meanwhile, he also gave them a steady diet of
imperialistic and republican sentiment.

Having provided Frenchmen their entertainment, Napo-
leon-the-Little hastened to consolidate his political power. By
the end of 1851 he struck. On December 1, all the opposition
members of the Assembly were arrested in their homes and
rushed to prison cells. Napoleon filled Paris with his troops
and the next morning announced that the Assembly was dis-
solved, that a new constitution had been promulgated that
made the presidential term of office ten years instead of four.
He then placed this before the people for ratification and the

French rushed to oblige. Less than a year later, by almost unanimous vote, they crowned their president Napoleon III, Emperor of France. French politics had now come full circle.

Few Frenchmen were astute enough to recognize what had happened to them. Bastiat had realized all along that Louis Napoleon was a man who calculated to do France great harm. Alexis de Tocqueville had believed some of the republican mouthings of Napoleon and had earlier accepted an appointment as minister of foreign affairs. However, when the Republic ended and the Empire began, Tocqueville realized his mistake and refused to take any further part in what he regarded as a conspiracy against France. Unfortunately, the Tocquevilles and the Bastiats were in short supply in the France of the 1850s.

Bastiat's Analysis of France in 1850

Even in the final laps of his race with death, Bastiat found time to analyze the French political scene and accurately predicted the end of republican government in France. During June of 1850, he retired to Mugron for a few days where he wrote the most famous and compelling of his books, *The Law*. In this work and in the other pamphlets and essays which he wrote during the last months of his life, Bastiat described why no society could hope to long endure under any political regime which denied freedom to its citizens:

> No society can exist if respect for the law does not to some extent prevail; but the surest way to have the laws respected is to make them respectable. When law and morality are in contradiction, the citizen finds himself in the cruel dilemma of either losing his moral sense or of losing respect for the law. . . .
> Unfortunately, the law is by no means confined to its proper

role. It is not only in indifferent and debatable matters that it has exceeded its legitimate function. It has done worse; it has acted in a way contrary to its own end; it has destroyed its own object: it has been employed in abolishing the justice which it was supposed to maintain, in effacing that limit between rights which it was its mission to respect; it has put the collective force at the service of those who desire to exploit, without risk and without scruple, the person, liberty, or property of others; it has converted plunder into a right, in order to protect it, and legitimate defense into a crime, in order to punish it.

Bastiat analyzed the interventionist society point by point and found it wanting in justice on every hand:

Alas? I find here so many nascent abuses, so many exceptions, so many direct or indirect deviations, appearing on the horizon of the new social order, that I do not know where to begin.

We have, first of all, licenses of all kinds. No one can become a barrister, a physician, a teacher, a broker, a dealer in government bonds, a solicitor, an attorney, a pharmacist, a printer, a butcher, or a baker without encountering legal restrictions. Each one of these represents a service that is forbidden by law, and hence those to whom authorization is granted raise their prices to such a point that the mere possession of the license, without the service, often has great value. . . .

Next comes the attempt to set an artificial price, to receive a supplementary value, by levying tariffs, for the most part on necessities: wheat, meat, cloth, iron, tools, etc. This is . . . a forcible violation of the most sacred of all property rights, that to the fruits of one's labor and productive capacities. . . .

Next comes taxation. It has become a much sought-after means of livelihood. We know that the number of government jobs has been increasing steadily, and that the number of applicants is increasing still more rapidly than the number of jobs. Now, does any one of these applicants ever ask himself whether he will render to the public services equivalent to those which he expects to receive? Is this scourge about to come to an end? How can we believe it, when we see that public opinion itself wants to have

everything done by that fictitious being, the state, which signifies
a collection of salaried bureaucrats? After having judged all men
without exception as capable of governing the country, we declare
them incapable of governing themselves. Very soon there will be
two or three of these bureaucrats around every Frenchman, one to
prevent him from working too much, another to give him an
education, a third to furnish him credit, a fourth to interfere with
his business transactions, etc., etc. Where will we be led by the
illusion that impels us to believe that the state is a person who has
an inexhaustible fortune independent of ours. . . . ?

I believe that we are entering on a path in which plunder, under
very gentle, very subtle, very ingenious forms, embellished with
the beautiful names of solidarity and fraternity, is going to assume
proportions the extent of which the imagination hardly dares to
measure. Here is how it will be done: Under the name of the state
the citizens taken collectively are considered as a real being, having
its own life, its own wealth, independently of the lives and the
wealth of the citizens themselves; and then each addresses this
fictitious being, some to obtain from it education, others employment, others credit, others food, etc., etc. Now the state can give
nothing to the citizens that it has not first taken from them. The
only effects of its intermediation are . . . a great dispersion of forces
. . . , for everyone will try to turn over as little as possible to the
public treasury and to take as much as possible out of it. In other
words, the public treasury will be pillaged. And do we not see
something similar happening today? What class does not solicit the
favors of the state? It would seem as if the principle of life resided
in it. Aside from the innumerable horde of its own agents, agriculture, manufacturing, commerce, the arts, the theatre, the colonies,
and the shipping industry expect everything from it. They want it
to clear and irrigate land, to colonize, to teach, and even to amuse.
Each begs a bounty, a subsidy, an incentive, and especially the
gratuitous gift of certain services, such as education and credit.
And why not ask the state for the gratuitous gift of all services?
Why not require the state to provide all the citizens with food,
drink, clothing, and shelter free of charge?

Bastiat warned that the price for viewing the law in this
way was high and that the perversion in political terms would

finally be a perversion of all social institutions as well, finally destroying society itself:

> The law is no longer the refuge of the oppressed, but the arm of the oppressor! The law is no longer a shield, but a sword! The law no longer holds a balance in its august hands, but false weights and false keys! And you want society to be well ordered!
>
> Your principle has placed these words above the entrance of the legislative chamber: "Whosoever acquires any influence here can obtain his share of legal plunder."
>
> And what has been the result? All classes have flung themselves upon the doors of the chamber, crying: "A share of the plunder for me, for me!"
>
> . . . And are you not appalled by the immense, radical, and deplorable innovation which will be introduced into the world on the day when the law itself is authorized to commit the very crime that it is its function to punish—on the day when it is turned, in theory and in practice, against liberty and property?
>
> You deplore the symptoms that modern society exhibits; you shudder at the disorder that prevails in institutions and ideas. But is it not your principle that has perverted everything, both ideas and institutions?

Thus Bastiat perceived the cycle. Undue government intervention in the lives of men inevitably produces legalized injustice, which leads to a lack of respect for the law, indeed for all authority and institutions. An immoral social order breeds immoral citizens. Soon the social fabric itself disintegrates. For societies as well as individuals, the wages of sin is death.

In failing health and in realization that the burden he had been carrying must pass to others, Bastiat left behind advice for those who would continue the struggle. He warned that political power was the cause of France's social decline and could never provide solutions to the problem. He asked that Frenchmen look outside the political arena and concluded:

". . . there is only one remedy: time. People have to learn, through hard experience, the enormous disadvantage there is in plundering one another." And this goes on until the people learn to recognize and defend their true interests.

The Race with Death

When a man has spent his first 45 years largely in solitude and quiet preparation, only a crisis that he regards as vitally important will cause him to leave that self-imposed isolation. For Bastiat, that crisis was the rampant socialism which so savagely attacked his native France. And the crisis was sufficiently pressing upon him that, once he had entered the fray, he drove himself unmercifully to devote all his energies to the task at hand. His last major work was to be *Economic Harmonies*, a sustained intellectual effort that literally consumed his life. The idea for *Economic Harmonies* had been growing on him for some years. He wrote to his old friend Coudroy about it in 1845, but two years later in the midst of his pressing duties in Paris, he was still struggling to find time to write the work he envisioned. Finally, in April of 1849 Bastiat wrote Coudroy that at last he was about ready to work out his theory in detail. One great idea filled his mind:

> Men's interests, rightly understood, are harmonious with one another, and the inner light that reveals them to men shines with an ever more vivid brilliance. Hence, their individual and collective efforts, their experience, their gropings, even their disappointments, their competition—in a word, their freedom—make men gravitate toward that unity which is the expression of the laws of their nature and the consummation of the common good.

Working feverishly, Bastiat poured forth his ideas. One can sense in the concluding chapter of *Harmonies* the desperate entanglement of thoughts that he had not the time to clearly organize and express. The book appeared early in 1850 and was treated coldly by the critics, even by many of Bastiat's former colleagues in the free trade movement. Undaunted, he began work on a second volume, which he was destined never to complete. Increasingly aware that he might not live to consummate his work, he speculated on the possibility of letting his old friend Coudroy finish the book, but decided that he and he alone could do the job that he wanted done. Bastiat simply lacked time to finish the work to his own satisfaction. Yet, the quality of his writing was such that today *Economic Harmonies* stands as a classic in its field.

It was also during these last months that Bastiat wrote the famous pamphlet, *What Is Seen and What Is Not Seen.* He had lost the entire manuscript during a period when he was relocating his household. After a careful but unsuccessful search, he decided that the pamphlet was of such importance that it deserved being done again. This second manuscript did not suit him, and he threw it into the fire. So, he wrote *What Is Seen and What Is Not Seen* for yet a third time.

To his old friend Richard Cobden, in August 1850, Bastiat wrote of his literary plans and his physical infirmities: "I went to my native country to try to cure these unfortunate lungs, which are to me very capricious servants. I have returned a little better, but afflicted with a disease of the larynx, accompanied with a complete extinction of voice. The doctor enjoins absolute silence; and, in consequence, I am about to pass two months in the country, near Paris."

He went on to tell Cobden some of his ideas for a second volume of *Economic Harmonies.* He also outlined another exciting idea that he never lived to develop:

An important task for political economy is to write the history of plunder. It is a long history involving, from the very beginning, conquests, migrations of peoples, invasions, and all the disastrous excesses of violence at grips with justice. All this has left an aftermath that still continues to plague us and that renders it more difficult to solve the problems of the present day. We shall not solve them so long as we are unaware of the way, and of the extent to which, injustice, present in our very midst, has gained a foothold in our customs and laws.

In these last days, sadness piled upon sadness for Bastiat. There had been a death in his family during his absence, he was now totally without political influence, no serious attention had been given to his most recent *Economic Harmonies*, and he was far too ill to fight back. A trip to the Pyrénées, a trip which had improved his bodily spirits several times in the past, this time only aggravated his illness. The infection which had spread to his throat began to disturb his digestion as well as his breathing.

In the fall of 1850, Bastiat was sent to Italy by his doctors. Arriving in Pisa, he read in the papers an announcement of his own death. Typically, he was amused at the references to "the great economist" and "the illustrious author." Writing to a friend to contradict the report, he said, "Thank God I am not dead, or even much worse. And yet if the news were true, I must just accept it and submit. I wish all my friends could acquire in this respect the philosophy I have myself acquired. I assure you I should breathe my last without pain, and almost with joy, if I were certain of leaving to the friends who love me, not poignant regrets, but a gentle, affectionate, somewhat melancholy remembrance of me."

From Pisa, Bastiat went on to Rome. Writing his old and

dear friend Coudroy for the last time, Bastiat discussed his plans for writing the second volume of *Economic Harmonies*. By Christmas Eve of 1850, Bastiat could go on no longer. At the last, he beckoned to those with him to approach the bedside. One of those present reported that ". . . his eye sparkled with that peculiar expression that I had frequently noticed in our conversations, and that announced the solution of a problem." Bastiat raised his head a bit as though to convey something of importance, and twice murmured the words, "The Truth." Then he was gone. Apparently Bastiat had solved one final problem to his satisfaction.

Some months before, Bastiat had written, "What gives me courage is . . . the thought that, perhaps, my life may not have been useless to mankind." For a man who had only been engaged in active public life for some six years, the balance sheet is indeed impressive. He had produced seven volumes of work, together with his service as a major political, social and economic commentator on his times. While he died too soon to realize that his ideas would have a lasting impact, the seeds he had sown would one day bear fruit. Bastiat's rediscovery in 20th-century America, a time and a place plagued by the same false ideas which so troubled his 19th-century France, is a clear indication that he has had a great impact, perhaps a greater impact than anyone appreciates.

CHAPTER 8

Bastiat and the Social Architects

What then, is the common denominator to which all forms of socialism are reducible, and what is the bond that unites them against natural society, or society as planned by Providence? There is none except this: They do not want natural society. What they do want is an artificial society, which has come forth full-grown from the brain of its inventor. . . . They quarrel over who will mold the human clay, but they agree that there is human clay to mold.

FREDERIC BASTIAT WAS FAR MORE THAN AN ECON-omist or a journalist. In his work there appears a grasp of the broadest social issues. In a modern world dominated largely by systems builders and planners, Bastiat has a great deal of importance as an antidote to the subtle poison contained in the idea that some social architects can mold the lives of men to the advantage of all.

Perhaps we should not be surprised that the 19th century spawned an unusually large number of social architects. The enormous changes of the Industrial Revolution—coupled with the political revolutions that had begun in France and that had swept through country after country in the Western world—had strongly impressed the idea of *change* upon the European mind. Since the changes that did occur were not only sweeping in nature, but were, presumably, changes for the better, the

idea of social reconstruction, of remodeling society in the aftermath of revolution, came to dominate the minds of many. The
idea of evolution, commonly discussed before Darwin and so
dear to 19th-century thinkers, also played its part in promot-
ing the idea of progress. Nineteenth-century thinkers tended
to see themselves living between the old and the new, groping
toward radical change, toward a new society, toward a new
world. Men had flirted with the idea of "progress" since the
time of the Greeks, but it was the men of the 19th century
who promoted progress into the be-all and end-all of society.

The rise of a new industrial working class channeled much
of the century's thinking into the confining intellectual framework of socialism. Building upon the anti-individualistic doctrines of Rousseau and the 18th-century *philosophes,* the social
architects came to feel that only collective and class-oriented
action on the part of the workers could produce the "progress"
which they felt awaited a properly planned society. Before the
theorists were through, they had produced the bloody revolutions of 1848. In the same year, Karl Marx spelled out the
doctrine of class struggle in the *Communist Manifesto,* urging
violence as not only necessary but desirable. For most of the
other social architects of Marx's generation, the course of action was far less clear. As one distinguished analyst of the
period, Louis Baudin, summarizes the era:

> 1840 to 1850 was such a characteristic era that history has given
> it a name: the "Forty Years." The storms of the Revolution and
> the Empire had calmed, leaving some dangerous backwaters. Roy-
> alty was fading with dignity, the Republic was not solidly built
> up and could not involve itself in the troubles and the ephemerals.
> Political parties mixed and battled furiously, the overthrown social
> classes searched for themselves among the debris of the divided and
> declining nobility. A new *bourgeoisie,* full of initiative and eager for

a profit, took shape, while a miserable and unsettled proletariat was born to a time of industrial revolution. . . .

The impartial observer has some difficulty finding himself in this storm. Excessiveness is the rule; the most absurd political theories find defenders, the most audacious politicians have their partisans. More passion than wisdom, more swagger than science, more flash than solidarity, many words, much protest, agitation, a grand romantic gust are the order of the day. . . . They [the social architects] sputtered words of promise and vague meanings: progress, socialism, sovereignty of the people.

The social architects had been at their work since the 18th century. Rousseau, the theorists of the French Revolution, Saint-Simon and Fourier, all these and others had paved the way for the social theorists who would disrupt France in the 1840s. Considérant, Blanc and Proudhon were well prepared to wage war on the social order, all in the name of Progress.

Bastiat recognized, far sooner than most men, the extreme dangers involved in the new politics and economics. Bastiat stood on particularly difficult ground since he could not pose as a defender of the old system under the French monarchy. In fact, Bastiat was a sharp critic of the old-style interventions in the lives of men, but he was also perceptive enough to see that the new-style interventions in the lives of men were an aggravation to social problems rather than an answer. Thus, Bastiat was forced to believe in progress. He could not urge a return to an earlier, happier day and had to meet the social architects on their own ground, granting their premise of an unfortunate past and yet pointing out the fallacies involved in their proposed utopias.

Fortunately, Frederic Bastiat brought to his difficult task both insight and humor. He was also unfailingly fair in his observations. Indeed, Bastiat's good humor and complete fairness in public controversy drove his opponents to distraction. It did not render him in any way unable to speak the truth in the most trenchant manner. He spoke plainly and frankly. Again and again he challenged the moral basis from which the social architects presumed to control the lives of other men. Bastiat directed his shafts at any and all who would manipulate society. In public debate, in books, in the press, Bastiat time after time crossed swords with virtually all of the prominent political and social thinkers of his age. In the process, he left a legacy of criticism which applies to the social architects of all times.

The Desire for Power

Bastiat probed the minds of the social architects and called attention to the almost total disagreement to be found among them:

> If I had to point out the characteristic trait that differentiates socialism from [a proper view of political economy], I should find it here. Socialism includes a countless number of sects. Each one has its own utopia, and we may well say that they are so far from agreement that they wage bitter war upon one another. Between M. Blanc's organized social workshops and M. Proudhon's anarchy, between M. Fourier's association and M. Cabet's communism, there is certainly all the difference between night and day. What then, is the common denominator to which all forms of socialism are reducible, and what is the bond that unites them against natural society, or society as planned by Providence? There is none except this: They do not want natural society. What they do want is an artificial society, which has come forth full-grown from the brain of its inventor. . . . They quarrel over who will mold the human clay, but they agree that there is human clay to mold. Mankind is not in their eyes a living and harmonious being endowed by God Himself with the power to progress and to survive, but an inert

mass that has been waiting for them to give it feeling and life; human nature is not a subject to be studied, but matter on which to perform experiments.

It was the recognition of that common trait of the social architects which caused Bastiat to mutter, "I still cannot understand why the numerous partisans of the systems opposed to liberty allow the word liberty to remain on the flag of the Republic."

Building upon his observation that the concern of the socialist was the development of an artificial social order, Bastiat stressed the point that the denial of the idea of a natural social order carried with it the denial that man's interests are fundamentally in harmony. Therefore, one of the prerequisites for destroying the natural order of society and substituting an artificial order in its place would be the necessity to demonstrate that men's interests are fundamentally antagonistic, one to another. Thus, the very nature of the social architect idea necessitated a belief that the property owner and the worker, capital and labor, the common people and the *bourgeoisie,* agriculture and industry, the farmer and the city dweller, the native born and the foreigner, the producer and the consumer, were all fundamentally in conflict, a conflict which must be furthered until the existing social order was destroyed in the process, thus removing all distinctions between and among men. For Bastiat, this explained how the social architects could profess to be filled to the brim with a love for humanity, yet constantly preach the doctrine of hatred.

The results for France were disastrous; indeed, the results for any country which listens to such prophets of hatred are always the same. Soon the poor rise against the rich, the proletariat against the capitalist, class against class. And when this happens, the social architects then tell us that conflict is the inevitable result of freedom. Substitute social organization and enforced brotherhood and all such conflict will pass away. Thus, those who have engineered our discontent now offer themselves as the only people who know how to bring it to an end.

And how brutal the enforced brotherhood. In the words of the revolutionaries in the France of the 1790s, "Be my brother or I shall kill thee." The social architects preach peace and war, harmony and disharmony, in the same breath, promising absolution from the human condition if we will only listen to them. Bastiat described Napoleon as a chemist who saw in Europe material for his experiment. He made it clear that the French revolutionaries of the 1790s, Napoleon, and the socialists who had followed in the 19th century, for all their bitter conflicts with one another, all shared the same essential view. He was fond of pointing out the fundamental contradiction involved:

> The demands of the socialists raise another question, which I have often addressed to them, and to which, as far as I know, they have never replied. Since the natural inclinations of mankind are so evil that its liberty must be taken away, how is it that the inclinations of the socialists are good? Are not the legislators and their agents part of the human race? Do they believe themselves molded from another clay than the rest of mankind? They say that society, left to itself, heads inevitably for destruction because its instincts are perverse.
>
> They demand the power to stop mankind from sliding down this fatal declivity and to impose a better direction on it. If, then, they have received from heaven intelligence and virtues that place them beyond and above mankind, let them show their credentials. They want to be shepherds, and they want us to be their sheep. This arrangement presupposes in them a natural superiority, a

claim that we have every right to require them to establish before we go any further.

Bastiat, of course, knew full well that the excuse of the social architects for assuming great power was that the power was in the hands of the state, for the good of all. As a benevolent and inexhaustible being, the state would provide ". . . bread for all mouths, work for all hands, capital for all enterprises, credit for all projects, ointment for all wounds, balm for all suffering, advice for all perplexities, solutions for all problems, truths for all minds, distractions for all varieties of boredom, milk for children and wine for old age," and thus become the agency ". . . which provides for all our needs, foresees all our desires, satisfies all our curiosity, corrects all our errors, amends all our faults, and exempts us all henceforth from the need for foresight, prudence, judgment, sagacity, experience, order, economy, temperance, and industry." It was Bastiat's great gift to be able to spell out the assumptions of the social architects so clearly and simply, leaving the absurdity to speak for itself. Yet, there lurked behind that absurdity the terrible truth that lies at the heart of all social planning: "If you start with the already absurd assumption that the government is the morally active force and that the nation is passive, are you not putting morals, doctrines, opinions, wealth, everything that makes up the life of the individual at the mercy of the men who one after another come to power?"

Rousseau

It is possible to discover in Bastiat's published works his analyses of the various fallacies that the social architects have displayed in their positions. Much of considerable import for our time can be gleaned from Bastiat's analyses of Rousseau, the architects of the French Revolution, Saint-Simon and Fourier, and the later social architects who were his contemporaries. In his analysis of the family tree of the socialist mentality, he penetrates to the heart of the problem. Convinced that Jean-Jacques Rousseau was the logical starting point for an analysis of the thinking dominating 19th-century France, Bastiat often discussed the 18th-century *philosophe* and his work. As he stated frankly in an 1848 article appearing in the *Journal des économistes:* "Rousseau was convinced that God, nature and man were wrong. I know that this opinion still sways many minds, but mine is not one of them."

Bastiat was extremely critical of Rousseau's idea that man was born in a state of nature and could only achieve true happiness by returning to that state. As he satirized Rousseau's position, ". . . man's true bliss is to be found in living in the woods, alone, naked, without ties, without affections, without language, without religion, without ideas, without family—in short, in a condition in which he was so little different from the beasts that it is really doubtful whether he stood upright and whether he did not have paws rather than hands." Rousseau, of course, had attacked property and social organization as the great dangers of mankind. For Bastiat, the opposition that Rousseau had set up between the state of nature and the state of society could only result in the denial of all justice and morality. In Rousseau's *Social Contract,* the *philosophe* had pursued the point even further, insisting that violation of the social contract allowed all parties to that contract to return to a state of "natural liberty," completely freed from any and all obligations to the social order. As Bastiat warned, the havoc which such a doctrine would wreak in an age of revolution was incalculable. In fact, the events of the French Revolution following 1789 were ample proof of how disastrous Rousseau's position could be.

Bastiat also faulted Rousseau for his insistence upon the *General Will,* a doctrine completely out of harmony with the "state of nature" position. In Rousseau's *General Will,* the future for the entire human race was to be found in subservience to a collective will of all men. The rights of private property and the guarantees of individual personality were to be swept aside and replaced with a collective *We,* operating under the care of the lawgiver, i.e., the social architect. Thus, Rousseau and many social revolutionaries since have said to the population, "Sweep aside all the restraints of property and society, destroy the existing system. Then you will be free, free to lose yourself in the collective good of mankind, under my care." In Bastiat's analysis of Rousseau's *Social Contract,* it is possible to see how a certain mentality can rebel against all authority at one moment and yet espouse the most socialist attitudes a moment later:

> Start with the idea that society is contrary to Nature; devise contrivances to which humanity can be subjected; lose sight of the fact that humanity has its motive force within itself; consider men as base raw materials; propose to impart to them movement at will, feeling and life; set oneself up apart, immeasurably above the human race—these are the common practices of the social planners. The plans differ; the planners are all alike. . . . Poor human race! What would the disciples of Rousseau do to your dignity?

The French Revolutionaries

Bastiat realized that the theoretical contradictions of Rousseau had been borne out in practice by the events of the French Revolution. In 1789, the old regime had been swept aside as repressive, just in time for the leaders of the Revolution to busy themselves in imposing a new and artificially planned society on the French people. Analyzing the words and actions of Saint-Just, Robespierre and the other revolutionaries, Bastiat made it clear that they were all in agreement concerning the necessity of dictatorship to promote virtue. In Robespierre's words, "The principle of republican government is virtue, and the means needed to establish it is terror." Bastiat spoke for all men in all ages when he analyzed Robespierre:

> At what a height above the rest of mankind Robespierre here places himself. And note the arrogance with which he speaks. He does not confine himself to expressing the wish for a great renovation of the human heart; he does not even expect such a result from a regular government. No, he wants to bring it to pass himself, and by means of terror. . . . Note that when Robespierre demands a dictatorship, it is . . . to make his own moral principles prevail by means of terror. . . . Oh, you wretches! You who believe yourselves so great! You who regard mankind as so inconsiderable! You want to reform everything! Reform yourselves first! This will be enough of a task for you.

Bastiat traced in great detail the assaults upon private property which had characterized the French Revolution. He pointed out that it had thrown aside all of the genuine guarantees of human freedom and personality, substituting the most brutal repressions in their place. He also reminded us that those repressions were invariably carried out in the name of "the people," as though there could be a public good arising from a private wrong.

Saint-Simon and Fourier

The madness begun in the French revolutionary era was destined to be nurtured and expanded in the 19th century. The Count Henri de Saint-Simon conceived a plan to make over France as a collectivist economy, under the control of technical experts. He insisted that man must be studied not as an individual, but en masse, and that all future social institutions must be organized around the masses. All this was to be done in the name of Christian ethics, as a part of a rather confused system of "the new Christianity."

Saint-Simon's disciples were given to the most bizarre ideas and activities. For a time, his followers dressed in a blue tunic with trousers to match and a scarlet jersey which buttoned at the back and which could not be undone except with the aid of some other person. The peculiar and impractical costume was intended to symbolize the mutual dependence of one man upon another. Such groups would sometimes go from place to place through out the country, and indeed even toured foreign countries, once reaching Constantinople, in a misbegotten missionary effort to convert the whole world to their new system.

François Fourier developed his own bizarre ideas and followers. For this particular social architect, cooperation was to replace competition as everyone left the exploitive industrial system to return to Rousseau's state of nature on cooperative farms. Though the Phalanxes, as the groups were called, sprang up throughout France and even spread to the United States, they were characterized more by strange ideas and actions than by lasting success.

At least such early utopians as Saint-Simon and Fourier did not feel it necessary to institute a revolutionary bloodbath against those choosing not to follow their direction. But the seeds of madness were present, nonetheless. The later social architects contemporary to Bastiat revealed a new urgency, a bitter impatience, that would one day convulse France in revolutionary outbursts.

Considérant

Bastiat engaged the social architects of his time individually and collectively. One of his more spectacular battles was his confrontation with Victor Considérant concerning the right of property. Bastiat published an analysis of Considérant's position that drew the ire of the man often characterized as "a Marxist before Marx."

Considérant had adopted the position that the right of employment was a right owed by society to all men, a right therefore enforceable by government. Bastiat had pointed out that such a "right" carried with it the threat of the destruction of all private property if government acted upon the notion. Considérant had posed as a defender of property, as a man wishing to make only a small change in the existing system in order to prevent unrest. He complained that Bastiat was misrepresenting his position, that his "right of employment" was only a necessary modification of the system to help it function more efficiently. How familiar that sounds today.

Pointing out that an attack upon the property rights of anyone finally amounted to an attack on the property rights of all men, Bastiat insisted that property was an extension of individual personality. Unless such extensions of self were guaranteed against the aggressions of the state, no matter how "humanitarian" those aggressions might be, the position of the individual within society would soon be untenable. Bastiat concluded his public demolition of the Considérant position: "If, then, M. Considérant is a tenacious defender of property, it is at least of a concept of property different from that which has been recognized and maintained among men since the beginning of the world. I am quite convinced that M. Louis Blanc and M. Proudhon also call themselves defenders of property as they understand it."

Blanc

Considerably more attractive to the French people, and therefore far more dangerous, were the ideas put forth by Louis Blanc. In a number of newspaper pieces, and in his book, *The Organization of Labor,* Blanc had insisted that the government had an obligation to guarantee employment to all able-bodied men. The idea of collective workshops had originated with him. Unalterably opposed to any form of competition, Blanc believed that his program would avoid the "exploitations" of the new industrial system and would also avoid class warfare.

For this reason, Blanc always fondly supposed that both workers and *bourgeoisie* would be attracted to his program. He believed that his new workshops would drive all private enterprise out of existence, and that mankind would now be happier in the planned community living which would develop around his workshops. One commentator has suggested that Blanc's bitter hatred of any superiority and his absolute insistence upon virtual equality of all men may have stemmed from some psychological need to assert himself the equal of all men, since, in physical stature, Louis Blanc was a dwarf.

Of all the ruthless leaders in mid-century France, Louis

Blanc was perhaps most popular, in part because his ideas were readily understandable and were contained within the simple slogan, "the right to employment." His popularity further rested on his reputation as an outspoken jingo. He urged a militant foreign policy on France to perpetuate the glories of the Napoleonic era. The discipline of the National Workshops and the discipline of the national armies apparently served a common purpose for Blanc.

Again and again, Blanc and Bastiat crossed swords. Each time, the specious arguments of Blanc suffered in the transaction:

> Do you not know that freedom means competition, and that competition, according to M. Louis Blanc, is a system of extermination for the common people, and a cause of ruin for the businessman? For evidence that the freer nations are, the closer they are to destruction and ruination, should we not look at Switzerland, Holland, England, and the United States [then easily the four most prosperous nations on earth]? Do you not know that, again according to M. Louis Blanc, competition leads to monopoly, and that, for the same reason, low costs lead to high prices? That competition tends to exhaust the sources of consumption and pushes production into a destructive activity? That competition forces production to increase and consumption to decrease? Whence it follows that free peoples produce in order not to consume—that liberty means both oppression and madness, and that M. Louis Blanc simply must step in and set matters straight?

Proudhon

Another of the social architects, Pierre Joseph Proudhon, is best known for his denunciation of private property as theft. His theories tend to run the gambit of 19th-century politics, so much so that he has been variously classified as both a philosophic anarchist and as a forerunner of fascism. Proudhon had no patience with the more popular Louis Blanc and even less patience with those who quoted "property is theft" by removing the remark from its full context. Proudhon was probably less radical than some of his fellow social planners. In fact, he preferred the American system in operation during the first half of the 19th century precisely because it governed least. For French politics, whether monarchist or republican, Proudhon had nothing but contempt. He suspected that the Louis Blancs of this world were little better than demagogues, and did not hesitate to say so.

At first glance, Proudhon might seem almost a sufficient maverick to stand with Bastiat against the currents of his time. However, Proudhon was so radical in his assumptions, and so quick to change his viewpoint, that some of his most bitter invective was reserved for controversy with Bastiat. When these two worthy antagonists met in the pages of the Paris newspapers, the clash resounded throughout France. The famous debate between the two men was first printed in the columns of Proudhon's paper, *The Voice of the People,* during 1849. Each man wrote one letter a week for twelve weeks. Proudhon's temper, never noted for stability, soon drove him beyond the bounds of polite discourse. Answering one of Bastiat's letters, Proudhon wrote: "Your intelligence sleeps, or rather it has never been awake. . . . You are a man for whom logic does not exist. . . . You do not hear anything, you do not understand anything. . . . You are without philosophy, without science, without humanity. . . . Your ability to reason, like your ability to pay attention and to make comparisons, is zero. . . . Scientifically, M. Bastiat, you are a dead man."

Proudhon's ill temper doubtless was provoked by the sound and persistent analysis which Bastiat brought to the debate.

Most of the published debate had centered on the moral, legal and economic justifications for the taking of interest. Bastiat, of course, defended the principle; Proudhon attacked it. Philosophically, Bastiat probably had the better of the debate. He certainly had the practical satisfaction of seeing Proudhon's "Bank of the People" (featuring cooperative exchange of goods and services, as well as interest-free loans) fail in 1849.

It should not be surprising that a classical liberal like Bastiat and an anarchist like Proudhon should agree on many points, but Proudhon saw paradox everywhere and could agree with no one for long. Bastiat regarded him as one of the dangerous men of the times:

> In recent times great pains have been taken to stir up public resentment against that infamous, that diabolical thing, capital. It is pictured to the masses as a ravenous and insatiable monster, more deadly than cholera, more terrifying than riots, as a vampire whose insatiable appetite is fed by more and more of the life-blood of the body politic. The tongue of this blood-sucking monster is called "rent," "usury," "hire," "service charges," "interest." A writer whose great talents could have made him famous had he not preferred to use them to coin the paradoxes that have brought him notoriety has seen fit to cast this paradox before a people already tormented by the fever of revolution.

Proudhon prided himself on the "discovery" that contradiction lies at the heart of all phenomena, that all institutions and ideas are hopelessly contradictory. Bastiat was sharply critical of that quality in Proudhon's thought and public behavior:

> God, a contradiction; liberty, a contradiction; property, a contradiction; value, credit, monopoly, common ownership, contradiction on contradiction! When M. Prouhon made this tremendous discovery, his heart must have surely leapt with joy; for since

contradiction is in all things, there is always something to contradict, which for him is the supreme happiness. He once said to me, "I'd be perfectly willing to go to heaven, but "I'm afraid everyone agrees up there, and I couldn't find anyone to argue with."

Bastiat warned that such men as Proudhon, who were introducing doubts about the function of capital into the minds of the French workers, were doing irreparable harm. Bastiat pointed out again and again that the progress of humanity coincided with the rapid formation of capital; he insisted that capital could not increase unless society were allowed to grow, and unless savings and security were possible. The working classes, according to him, "must learn that capital has from the beginning of time worked to free men from the yoke of ignorance, want and tyranny. To frighten away capital is to rivet a triple chain around the arms of the human race."

CHAPTER 9

Bastiat and the Whig and Liberal Traditions

To tamper with man's freedom is not only to injure him, to degrade him; it is to change his nature, to render him, in so far as such oppression is exercised, incapable of improvement; it is to strip him of his resemblance to the Creator, to stifle within him the noble breath of life with which he was endowed at his creation.

IN BASTIAT'S REACTION TO THE THINKING OF HIS time, we see a man drawing upon the thoughts of some of his predecessors, while projecting ideas which others would use later in the 19th century. Locke, Smith, Burke, Coleridge, Bentham, Mill—these and others are echoed or anticipated in Bastiat. Thus Bastiat forms a vital link in our understanding of the strengths and weaknesses contained in the philosophy which men offer in opposition to the omnipotent state.

The only means of penetrating the twisted trail of "conservative-libertarian" thought as reflected in Bastiat is a consideration of several generations of British and French thinkers. Such an examination of one's intellectual forebears is well worth the effort, though it is unlikely to provide the simplistic answers so beloved of all doctrinaires, whether communist, socialist, liberal, conservative, or libertarian. Indeed one of the strongest arguments of those who value freedom is the insistent idea that human endeavor cannot be encompassed within any philosophy which divorces itself from reality, no matter whose it might be. A bit of complexity may be good for the soul. Be that as it may, it is absolutely essential to an understanding of Frederic Bastiat and his significance.

The Whig Tradition

One of the most effective treatments of the Whig tradition in history appears in the work of the 20th-century classical economist Friedrich Hayek. In *The Constitution of Liberty,* Hayek traces the development of the Whig emphasis upon individual liberty to 17th-century England, where the new emphasis upon freedom appeared more as the "by product of a struggle for power rather than as the result of deliberate aim." He credits the Middle Ages for their contribution to the idea of freedom, but looks primarily to the Glorious Revolution of 1688 and to John Locke's speculations about the philosophical foundations of government as the real source of the Whig tradition:

> While in his philosophical discussion Locke's concern is with the source which makes power legitimate and with the aim of government in general, the practical problem with which he is concerned is how power, whoever exercises it, can be prevented from becoming arbitrary: "Freedom of men under government is to have a standing rule to live by, common to every one of that society, and made by the legislative power erected in it; a liberty to follow my own will in all things, where that rule prescribes not: and not to be subject to the inconstant, uncertain, arbitrary will of another man." It is against the "irregular and uncertain exercise of the power" that the argument is mainly directed: the important point is that "whoever has the legislative or supreme power of any commonwealth is bound to govern by established standing laws

promulgated and known to the people, and not by extemporary decrees; by indifferent and upright judges, who are to decide controversies by those laws; and to employ the forces of the community at home only in the execution of such laws." Even the legislature has no "absolute arbitrary power," "cannot assume to itself a power to rule by extemporary arbitrary decrees, but is bound to dispense justice, and decide the rights of the subject by promulgated standing laws, and known authorized judges," while the "supreme executor" of the law . . . has no will, no power but that of the law . . . his ultimate aim throughout is what today is often called the "taming of power": the end why men "choose and authorize a legislative is that there may be laws made, and rules set, as guards and fences to the properties of all the members of society, to limit the power and moderate the dominion of every part and member of that society."

However much the Whig ideas of John Locke had gained popular acceptance by the beginning of the 18th century, it is in the development of public policy in 18th-century England that we see the ideas gradually put into effect. The Whigs increasingly implemented a system of limited government favorable to individual liberty, described in Hayek's *The Road to Serfdom* as "The Rule of Law." The Whigs were never very explicit in the delineation of their ideas. Something in the empirical and non-doctrinaire British mind mitigated against any precise formulation. Perhaps the Whig position could best be described as an attempt to free men from the caprices of political control.

Later in the 18th century these ideals are more often taken for granted than explicitly stated, and the modern reader has to infer them when he wants to understand what men like Adam Smith and his contemporaries meant by "liberty." Only occasionally, as in Blackstone's *Commentaries,* do we find endeavors to elaborate particular points, such as the significance of the independence of the judges and of the separation of powers, or to clarify the meaning of "law" by its definition as "a rule, not a transient sudden order from a superior or concerning a particular person; but something permanent, uniform and universal."

Burke

Though Whigs such as Adam Smith did not spell out in detail what they meant by "liberty," there can be little doubt that their thinking was strongly oriented toward individual freedom, as protected by the "Rule of Law." Certainly in the work of Edmund Burke the tradition is given a statement which is unmistakable. Burke was writing in response to the events of the French Revolution. He saw the events following 1789 as a violent overthrow of all the guarantees of private property and individual liberty upon which the Whig tradition was based. Burke is generally regarded as the founder of modern conservatism since he resisted the rationalist contempt for the past and enunciated the necessity for strong and deep ties with tradition. He spoke for the aristocratic and freedom-oriented Whig landowners of his time. *Reflections on the Revolution in France* was published in 1790. From beginning to end it is a ringing indictment of the rationalist position. Burke savagely attacked the idea that men could generate a perfect society through some mad scheme which would overturn all existing order. He spoke as strongly against the social architects of his day as Bastiat did in France five decades later.

Edmund Burke saw the Whig Revolution of 1688 as "a revolution not made, but prevented," describing the revolution which overthrew James II as an attempt to preserve the institutions, laws, and liberties of England, with its traditional concerns for the individual and for the guarantees for private property. He contrasted the Whig Revolution of 1688 with the French Revolution of 1789 and its resultant destruction, terror and anarchy. Earlier, Burke had been sympathetic to the American Revolution of 1776, which he described as an attempt to preserve the rights of property and the freedoms of individuals against the attacks of government. In fact, Burke and many of the distinguished Whigs of his time had spoken up in defense of the American Revolution during the critical years when the colonies were winning their independence.

Burke and the Whigs had also consistently championed the liberties of the mind. In speech after speech before Parliament, Burke had defended freedom of speech (1771), religious freedom (1773), and all guarantees of individual action against the overweening power of government. In Burke, the essentially libertarian nature of political and economic conservatism at its best is readily apparent.

Frenchmen and Englishmen

Burke's reaction to the French Revolution crystalized two views of human freedom and the means to its attainment. The British view, unsystematic and based upon the preservation of past traditions and institutions of freedom, is clearly at odds with the French view, which is rationalist, given to flattering presuppositions about the perfectibility of human nature and prone to the construction of utopian societies. The English school of thought can be seen quite clearly in the Whigs, Adam Smith and Edmund Burke. The French *philosophes* and Physiocrats epitomize the French tradition. It should be emphasized that men on both sides of the Channel believed in human freedom; it was in their underlying philosophic assumptions that the enormous differences lay. If the British tradition would honor the past, the French would sweep it away in a torrent of change. If the French would construct a utopia, the English would distrust all closet philosophies not hammered out on the anvil of experience. If the English tradition would take human nature as it found it, the French would assume that man was perfectible. If the French were prone to speak of Man, the English preferred to speak of individual men, each one a unique person.

It would be misleading to assume that all Frenchmen subscribed to the French school of thought. Alexis de Tocqueville evidenced deep roots in the English tradition of liberty. By the same token, many English intellectuals of the 18th and 19th centuries were entirely in the French rationalist camp: Priestley, Paine and Bentham are clear cases in point. The great division between the two positions lay in their respective views of civilization. For the French school of liberty, civilization was raw material to be fashioned according to the philosopher's whims. For the English school of liberty, civilization was the accumulation of centuries of trial and error, a tender growth not to be discarded lightly for anyone's utopian plans.

Coleridge

Like many of the outstanding literary men of his generation, Samuel Taylor Coleridge at first had been strongly attracted to the French Revolution and its utopian goal of sweeping away all Man's corruption to replace it with the perfect society. The excesses of the Revolution soon brought a reaction. By 1798, Coleridge had discovered that the sweeping utopian vision of the perfect society led only to an even more bitter slavery than the French people had suffered before:

> When France in wrath her giant-limbs upreared, . . . Stamped her strong foot and said she would be free, Bear witness for me, how I hoped and feared! . . ./ The Sensual and the Dark rebel in vain, Slaves by their own compulsion!/ In mad game They burst their manacles and wear the name of freedom,/ graven on a heavier chain!

Coleridge well understood that human happiness depended upon more than mere political forms. Instead, he emphasized inner, spiritual change, automatically suspecting the ruthless, secular, materialistic society that the rationalist planner was likely to create. He understood full well the necessity for inner growth of the individual as the only lasting means of social progress:

> One good consequence which I expect from [disillusionment with] revolution is that individuals will see the necessity of individual effort; that they will act as good Christians, rather than as citizens and electors; and so by degrees will purge off . . . the error of attributing to governments a talismanic influence over our virtues and our happiness, as if governments were not rather effects than causes.

Bentham

If Coleridge epitomized the English tradition of liberty, his fellow Englishman and contemporary Jeremy Bentham epitomized the French rationalist tradition. For Bentham, founder of Philosophic Radicalism, civilization was merely a large room filled with the furniture of social institutions, to be moved about and refashioned in whatever manner most likely to produce the ideal society. While it is true that Bentham attacked the ideology of the French Revolution, one wonders if he did not do so primarily because he distrusted the work of the French National Assembly, and would have preferred to have done the planning himself. There can be no doubt that Jeremy Bentham possessed a sentimental faith in human perfectibility, and in abstract rationalist philosophy to achieve that perfection. He reasoned to his conclusions about society from an *a priori* assumption, basing his celebrated calculus of pain and pleasure upon an abstract view of Man which saw no higher value in society than to maximize pleasure and minimize pain.

It is true that Bentham was a pronounced individualist in his economic philosophy, but his espousal of *laissez faire* was always based upon the grounds of utility. Thus, it was only a matter of time until the utilitarian position, with no underlying principle to guide it, would be led by its calculus of pleasure and pain toward egalitarian economics as a means of reducing pain and increasing pleasure. The connection between the utilitarianism of Jeremy Bentham and the Fabian socialism which came to dominate English society several generations later is far more immediate and direct than is generally recognized. Bentham and the Fabians were all too willing to regard men as little more than animals requiring a keeper. The great political struggle which took place in 19th-century England was essentially between the followers of the French rationalist tradition and the great Whig landowners. The Benthamites and the rest of the philosophic radicals triumphed in the end, and with that triumph expired the last best hope of saving liberalism from the clutches of rationalist, *a priori* reasoning.

It is true that Bentham and those who followed his line of thinking—most notably John Stuart Mill—were libertarians in the sense that they believed men to be more productive (and thus happier, in the pleasure-pain calculus) when society was free. But the *a priori* assumption at the root of their view of men envisioned a society sufficient unto itself, a society which could remake civilization and human nature as required, with no concern for a moral framework and no necessity for a faith in God. A system which thus leaves God out of its calculations tends to become dry as dust and in time opens the door to a new calculus—the horror of modern "ism"s which willingly enslave men in a quest to make them happy. Those who base their appeals exclusively on material progress, preaching endlessly about the number of refrigerators, automobiles and flush toilets in our modern society, partake of the same error. The old pleasure-pain calculus thus rears its ugly head once again, obscuring and sometimes denying the infinitely more important moral point which underlies the case for freedom. In the process, it is small wonder that such crass materialism antagonizes many who otherwise would be attracted to the freedom ideal.

Mill

Readers of John Stuart Mill's *On Liberty* may take issue with anyone attempting to characterize him as the connection between Jeremy Bentham and the Fabian Socialists. Surely the author of *On Liberty* must be a believer in human freedom. Mill is an interesting case in point precisely because he could be simultaneously an apostle of individual freedom and a link in the process of degradation whereby liberalism became synonymous with socialism. He epitomizes better than any other thinker of his time the peculiar dichotomy destined to destroy the emphasis upon freedom within modern liberalism.

Mill had earlier examined the thought of Samuel Taylor Coleridge and Jeremy Bentham and had quite properly criticized Bentham for his belief that all human affairs could be reduced to a few tidy philosophic abstractions. Unfortunately, in his later work Mill fell into the same fatal trap. Before his death, he had become a socialist. He came to talk endlessly about "economic man," as though man could be separated by the rationalist into a series of component parts, to be analyzed, remodeled and reassembled according to "the greatest utility." Liberalism, divorced from its sound Whig roots in Adam Smith and Edmund Burke, was destined to slip into the same rationalist assumption that society could be remade according to abstract humanitarian principles. The rationalism of Bentham and Mill was destined to become the Fabianism of Shaw and the Webbs.

Cobden

Richard Cobden was another of the key personalities who played a large role in transforming Whiggism into liberalism. Cobden's thought centered exclusively around the idea of free trade. Although his Anti-Corn Law League stressed the class conflict between the Whig landowners and the rising commercial interests, Cobden preferred to think of free trade as a law of nature, as a concept which society could reject only at its great peril. He saw the struggle against the great Whig landlords as a struggle against feudal limitations, as an attempt to substitute freedom and competition for all men in place of privilege and political intervention in favor of a few. He was so sure that free trade would solve all England's problems and thus benefit all Englishmen that he felt himself a defender of the old England, the England of the small landowner. Richard Cobden was trying to conserve traditional English society as he saw it, even though his principal opponents were the Whig landowners who had been the traditional defenders of English freedoms. In Cobden we see something of Burke's impulse to conserve, plus something of the rationalist enthusiasm for the perfect society.

This peculiar Cobden mixture of conservative and liberal, traditionalist and rationalist, was further compounded by a strong middle-class emphasis. Karl Marx was never more class-conscious than Richard Cobden. The group on which he pinned all his hopes for the salvation of society was the emerging middle class, the same group fated to give disastrous mismanagement to French political affairs between 1830 and 1848. Cobden totally rejected the Whig politics of the preceding 150 years, referring to it as "the worst thing that ever befell this country." He seemed to envision the perfect industrial society in which the industrious middle classes were destined to make modern England the envy of all the world.

In this way, Cobden was a utilitarian in the narrowest possible sense of the word. He tended to measure all social progress by middle class material standards. In the process, the older Whig conservatism gave way to the newer style liberalism of Jeremy Bentham: "Make men prosperous and they will be happy." Cobden also epitomized the new liberalism in his emphasis upon John Stuart Mill's compartmentalization of man into his political and economic functions. As in Bentham and Mill and the rest of the 19th-century British liberals, Cobden's thought always tended to make too little of men by reducing them to such compartmentalized abstractions. This is harder to see in Cobden than in some of the other liberals, because he possessed certain homey intellectual vices which they did not, notably his preoccupation with the "solid and industrious middle class." In Cobden, as in the others of his generation, it is easy to find much with which we are sympathetic, but it is well to remind ourselves that their ideas contained the seeds from which modern democratic socialism would one day grow.

Cobbett

If the liberals of 19th-century England were beginning to show the shortcomings of their intellectual position, the conservatives were doing little better. The social questions involved in what shall be conserved and how it shall be conserved are among the most difficult in Christendom. The Whigs had conserved many of the institutions and traditions of individual freedom, but in the process they had also conserved their own privileges as feudal landowners. The attempted reforms of Bentham, Mill and Cobden had been liberal in intent, yet had thrown out the baby with the bath and had paved the way for liberalism to become Fabian socialism.

Meanwhile, some Englishmen were attempting to "conserve" portions of the English past that were already dead, and in the process were also helping to discredit freedom, albeit in their own special way. William Cobbett, the English journalist, politician and pamphleteer, is an obvious case in point. He was fond of talking about the simple, hearty life of the traditional English yeoman, centering on good drink, good food and hard labor. For Cobbett, the 19th century was an uncomfortable time: everything was in a state of flux around him. He hated the machinery of the Industrial Revolution. He hated the idea of progress because it was breaking up the old fixed loyalties of England. Cobbett was so conservative that he became England's leading radical. He hated the new order so much that he was led to attack the important remaining portions of the old order. If Bentham and the utilitarians foresaw a materialist paradise on the road ahead, Cobbett was traveling the same road, though headed in the opposite direction. For that reason, Jeremy Bentham and William Cobbett, the would-be liberal and the would-be conservative, both looked to parliamentary reform and increasing political democracy as a means of achieving their diametrically opposed ends.

William Cobbett was a conservative of conservatives in his bitter opposition to the French Revolution and everything it stood for, yet so little understood its significance that he later came to view the Revolution as essentially beneficial, since it had destroyed Bourbon aristocracy, and "returned the French soil to the peasants." However incorrect and wrong-headed such wishful thinking might be concerning the actual events of the French Revolution, Cobbett was true to form in his response. He was never able to understand that "giving all political power to the people" might breed a new tyranny even more reprehensible than the old. For this reason, he led the way for political reform in England, playing a major role in the passage of the Reform Bill of 1832. Talking endlessly about the "rights of man" as a basis for his electoral reform, Cobbett never made the connection between such rationalist abstractions and the "Progress" to which he objected. He spoke with hatred of the materialist emphasis of the manufacturers coming to dominate England, and failed to realize that the whole basis of the political revolution he was helping to bring about hinged upon political exploitation of those same material appetites among the lower classes.

Wishing to see the common people of England restored to

the status of an earlier day ("I wish to see the poor men of England what the poor men of England were when I was born"), he believed that political means would conserve these values. Unfortunately for his peace of mind, he lived to see Parliament pass the new Poor Law, guaranteeing the final destruction of that hardy-yeoman independence of which he was so proud.

He was so desperately concerned with his misguided crusade that he finally came even to deny the property right, since some men had come to possess so much property that the balance of the older British society, which he presumably wished to conserve, had now been upset. For him the expropriation of property became a device by which traditional British society would be "conserved." He looked back with approval to the medieval prohibition of interest and loathed the whole financial system of credit and paper money. He hated the new order so bitterly that he was quite prepared to use massive political intervention to solve all problems. The result was not the conservation of Cobbett's beloved earlier English society, but the further destruction of British liberties which had centered on private property and the individual.

England Loses Her Way

By mid-century, English conservatives had forgotten what they were conserving. English liberals had forgotten what freedom meant, and the Whigs were dead beyond recall. The first 50 years of the 19th century had witnessed a steady decline in the institutions and ideas of freedom in England. As Hayek describes the change in *The Constitution of Liberty:* "Bentham and his Utilitarians did much to destroy the beliefs which England had in part preserved from the Middle Ages by their scornful treatment of most of what until then had been the most admired features of the British constitution. And they introduced into Britain what had so far been entirely absent— the desire to remake the whole of her law and institutions on rational principles."

Perhaps we expect too much of Burke and the Whigs when we wonder why they were so unsuccessful in stemming the decline of individual freedom. Surely Burke faced formidable obstacles. He was confronted with an Industrial Revolution which carried with it the steadily rising material expectations of all classes. That these rising expectations should be vented through political channels, that political power could be used to plan the new technological utopia, seemed "self-evident" to several generations of Englishmen. We should not be surprised that English political life took such a direction. The Whigs suffered from another great disadvantage in their struggle for freedom: All political power was shifting from Whig landowners to the new manufacturers, financiers, and merchants. The Industrial Revolution was generating its new ruling class.

Not surprisingly, the new ruling class brought with it middle class democracy. The same currents which Bastiat so criticized in France between 1830 and 1848 were being felt in England as well. And, as Bastiat pointed out, if the political manipulation of human affairs is desirable for middle-class interests, why not political regulation of human affairs in the interests of the lower classes? Soon the contest for political power would dominate society.

The prophets of the new order must also bear a share of the blame. The open-ended society of Adam Smith, favoring freedom as primarily a *moral* goal, and viewing prosperity as an incidental accompanying blessing gave way to a growing materialism in the thinking of the later Manchester School. In Ricardo and Malthus, it seemed plain that the producer become subject to production, and men became subject to things. The "Iron Law" of the new system not only whetted the appetite of the new industrial Europe, but also paved the way for reaction against the system. If the Iron Law were indeed so immutable, then surely political power must be exercised to redress the balance. If the ultimate human values are material in nature why not exercise political power to share this bounty? After Adam Smith, the substitution of the material for the moral robbed the Manchester School of its basis of principle upon which a stand could be made.

Jeremy Bentham and his followers epitomized the new order. They reflected a political faith dominantly middle class and oriented toward technology, the Industrial Revolution, and the development of what today would be called "political administration." The Reform Act of 1832 was the first major step bringing about the desired political change. *Bourgeois* politics came into its own in the England of 1832 in a manner surprisingly similar to the Revolution of 1830 in France. Changes in both countries were equally revolutionary, with the only real difference centering on the characteristically English capacity for peaceful change and the seeming French necessity for violent change. The middle classes in both countries had high hopes: surely modern democratic politics had arrived, sweeping away privilege and replacing it with solid material values and technological progress for all.

After 1832, the Chartist agitation began to bring pressure to bear for a further expansion of the franchise to include the English working classes. This was a tide that could no more be stopped in England than in France. Once the old aristocracy and the *bourgeoisie* had begun to play class politics, one could rest assured that the working class would not long tolerate exclusion from the game. Marx was not far wrong in his assumption of class struggle; his mistake was that he did not expect the struggle to be fought out for political benefits during a democratic regime.

As the 19th century reached its mid-point, it became clear that all shades of political opinion wished to play a role as the architects of a new England, with the remodeling process empowered by political pressures. People who called themselves conservatives wished to use political power to reverse the forces of change. People who called themselves liberals and utilitarians wished to use political power to speed the process of change. Those who recognized that interventions of political power in the lives of men were likely to have negative consequences were few in number, far from the seats of influence, and nameless.

Of course, the new social radicalism of the middle classes did not proceed rapidly enough for those who urged total and immediate reform. The new generation of politicians, sensing the direction of change, courted the favor of the aroused population promising more and more in material benefits, and demanding less and less individual responsibility. England lagged only a few years behind France's timetable for the chaos which Bastiat fought in his last year. In England the parties took the names of Whig and Tory, but the new style Whig and Tory were preaching the same doctrine to such an amazing extent that little real difference could be distinguished. The Whigs under Brougham had faint connection with the party of Burke. The Tories under Disraeli gave much lip service to tradition, but carried through the most radical "social reforms" in 19th-century England. Surely the electoral reform of 1867, which took place under Tory direction, was the final blow to any limitation on the political process, much as the Revolution of 1848 had been the final blow in France. No amount of Disraeli's rhetoric in praise of "tradition" can disguise that fact.

A few of the old-style friends of liberty remained on the scene, notably Sir Henry Maine, whose *Popular Government* was published in 1885. He applied the Burkean approach to the problems of 19th-century industrialism and warned that liberty and equality were essentially incompatible. Liberty and civilization, both so deeply entangled with the concept of private property and individual rights, simply could not exist under a socialist tyranny, even though it chanced to be a "tyranny of the majority." Maine accurately predicted the course of modern democracy in virtually every country in the Western world when he wrote: "By a wise constitution, democracy may be made nearly as calm as water in a great artificial reservoir; but if there is a weak point anywhere in the structure, the mighty forces which control it will burst. . . ."

The American Whig

Maine, Burke, Tocqueville, Bastiat, and others had been quick to notice one nation that seemed bent upon giving the fullest possible development to the ideals of limited government and protected private property rights as the guarantors of individual freedom. The United States was the one outstanding example of how these ideals could operate in practice. The American Revolution had come about primarily because England had insisted on interfering with the political and economic freedom of the thirteen colonies. Burke and the Whigs of his time had warmly supported the American cause. The support was reciprocated as the Americans perceived that most of the guiding notions of the new republic had their origins deep in established Whig principles of limited government and the rule of law.

Unfortunately, the American use of the term "Whig" as it developed in the 19th century degenerated into a label for a party of political hacks, much as the name had degenerated in England. Despite this, Whig principles lived on for the remainder of the century. Often the student of American history is asked to choose between the alleged radicalism of Jefferson and the alleged conservatism of Hamilton, but the animating spirit of the 19th century—at its best—lay in the ideas of James Madison, America's best version of a traditional Whig statesman. The ideals of the free market and the limited state were so deeply embedded in the colonial and early republican experience in America that it took much longer for the corruptions of the modern "equalitarian democracy" to erode the system.

Taine and Tocqueville

If Bastiat had few allies abroad, he had even fewer at home. One of the few, however, was the distinguished historian Hippolyte Taine. In his scholarship, Taine played the same role as Sir Henry Maine in England. He insisted that centralization was destroying French democracy. But, more than any other contemporary, it was Alexis de Tocqueville who shared Bastiat's bitter opposition to the political and economic trends in mid-19th century France. Tocqueville was more likely to stress tradition and established historical forms of freedom, while Bastiat's arguments were based on freedom as an abstract principle, and as a law of nature.

Yet the parallels between the two men are numerous. Not

only did their lifespans closely coincide, but they spent the majority of their lives in quiet study and retirement from the world. Both had a brief, but important careers in public life at the height of political turbulence. Both came to the same disturbing conclusions that politicians would be unable to defend the principles of limited government and protected private property rights. Tocqueville summed up the fears of both when he wrote: "Before long the political struggle will be restricted to those who have and those who have not, property will form the great field of battle; and the principal political questions will turn upon the more or less important modifications to be introduced into the right of property. We shall then have once more great political agitations and great [divisive] political parties."

CHAPTER 10

Frederic Bastiat Today

We see, then, that in almost all of the important actions
of life we must respect men's free will, defer to their own
good judgment, to that inner light that God has given
them to use, and beyond this to let the law of responsibility take its course.

THERE ARE A NUMBER OF AREAS IN WHICH WE CAN
still learn a great deal from Bastiat, in both economic and
political terms. In economics, Bastiat made a number of telling points which have direct application in contemporary debate.

The Seen and the Unseen

One of these areas is Bastiat's consistent emphasis upon "the
seen and the unseen." Here, in a brilliant flash of insight,
Bastiat put his finger on one of the prime fallacies in economic
thinking that still haunts the modern world:

In the economic sphere an act, a habit, an institution, a law
produces not only one effect, but a series of effects. Of these effects,
the first alone is immediate; it appears simultaneously with its
cause; it is seen. The other effects emerge only subsequently; they
are not seen; we are fortunate if we foresee them.
There is only one difference between a bad economist and a
good one: the bad economist confines himself to the visible effect;

141

the good economist takes into account both the effect that can be seen and those effects that must be foreseen.

Yet this difference is tremendous; for it almost always happens that when the immediate consequence is favorable, the later consequences are disastrous, and vice versa. Whence it follows that the bad economist pursues a small present good that will be followed by a great evil to come, while the good economist pursues a great good to come, at the risk of a small present evil.

Does government spending stimulate the economy? The effects that are seen would seem to prove that it does. But the effect that is not seen is that government cannot spend money that it does not take from the taxpayer in one form or another. As a result, what is not seen is that government can only give to people a portion of what it has already taken from them. What productive miracles might have been wrought had government taxation and inflation not distorted the picture?

We Are All Consumers

It is said that four days before Bastiat's death, with his mind still racing to record every possible insight that he could discover, he advised future economists, "... to treat economic questions always from the consumer's point of view, for the interest of the consumer is identical with that of mankind." Bastiat felt that the most severe error in economic thinking stemmed from a failure to recognize that consumption is the end and final cause of all economic phenomena. He pointed out that the consumer becomes richer in proportion as he buys more cheaply, that he buys more cheaply as goods become more abundant, and that abundance is produced by allowing the fullest possible production. Thus all laws designed to interfere with the productive miracle are eventually laws punishing the consumer. Stressing the enormous interdependence of all men in the marketplace, emphasizing the fact that the farmer does not make his own clothes, the tailor does not raise the wheat that he consumes, and so on for the countless other benefits that we all daily derive from the marketplace, Bastiat insisted that the enormous saving in time and effort that came about from division of labor and free exchange provided a system in which the more effective producer was the strongest possible ally of the consumer. He pointed out that the man who profited from the low cost and ready availability of a product was the man who consumed it. Attempts to interfere with that relationship would inevitably prove to be defeating for society as a whole:

> If you wish to prosper, let your customer prosper. This is a lesson it has taken you a very long time to learn.
>
> When people have learned this lesson, everyone will seek his individual welfare in the general welfare. Then jealousies between man and man, city and city, province and province, nation and nation, will no longer trouble the world.

Production of True Wealth

Asking the rhetorical question, "Which is preferable for man and for society, abundance or scarcity?" Bastiat stressed a point that modern society still does not understand: "Wealth consists in an abundance of commodities." When we persist in regulating the number of competitors that can enter the marketplace, limiting the number of hours that a man may work, manipulating the wages and prices that may be charged, we demonstrate our absurd belief that limiting men's freedom to produce and compete will somehow make us all wealthier. Of course, every limitation exacts its toll from the marketplace, and ultimately from each consumer. There is no difference in principle between a tariff, a regulatory commission, or any other variety of present-day interventionism, and Bastiat's facetious suggestion that candlemakers and their allied industries should receive government protection against the unfair competition of the sun.

With Bastiat, we might ask, ". . . are we to believe that the people are better fed under the laws that prevail at present, because there is less bread, meat, and sugar in the country? Are they better clad, because there is less linen and woolen cloth? Are their houses better heated, because there is less coal? Is their labor made easier, because there is less iron and copper, or because there are fewer tools and machines?"

Restrictive laws always present us with the same dilemma. Either we admit that they produce scarcity, or we do not admit it. If we do admit it, we thereby confess that they inflict upon the people all the harm that they can do. If we do not admit it, then we deny that they limit the supply of goods and raise their prices, and consequently we deny that they favor the producer. Such laws are either injurious or ineffective. They cannot be useful.

The Necessity of Capital

In an age when capital and labor were assumed to be antagonistic, Bastiat pointed out that capital and labor cannot get along without each other. He urged the freest and most voluntary transactions between capital and labor, and warned that any intervention on behalf of one against the other was likely to produce results which would penalize all.

Bastiat insisted that absolute poverty had been the starting point for mankind, and that the only possible road upward from general poverty was through the formation of capital, of savings put to productive use, savings making the skills of the individual worker far more productive than they would otherwise be. Speaking to an age almost as blind to this relationship as our own, Bastiat warned the French worker:

> The questions for the worker to ask himself are not: "Does my labor bring me a great deal? Does it bring me very little? Does it bring me as much as it brings another? Does it bring me what I should like?"
>
> Rather, he should ask: "Does my labor bring me less because I have put it at the service of the capitalist? Would it bring me more if I performed it on my own, or if I joined my labor with that of others as destitute as I am? My situation is bad. Would I be better off if there were no capital on earth? If the share that I receive as a result of my arrangement with capital is larger than my share would be without it, what grounds do I have for complaint? And then, if transactions are free and voluntary, what are the laws determining whether there is to be a rise or a fall in the amount of our respective shares? If the nature of these transactions is such that, as the total to be distributed increases, my share in the increase becomes steadily larger, then, instead of vowing eternal hatred against the capitalist, ought I not to look upon him as a good brother? If it is well established that the presence of capital is advantageous to me, and that its absence would mean my death, am I very wise or prudent in abusing it, intimidating it, requiring it to be frittered away or forcing it into hiding?
>
> If fishermen would prefer to fish without the boats and nets which belong to another, or if workers would prefer to work without the machines which belong to a capitalist, let them do so. When the situation is phrased in this way, it demonstrates the utter absurdity of anti-capitalist political interventions, interventions presumably designed to aid the workers.

The truly democratic feature of the new industrial order rested partially upon the greatly increased production which modern capitalism made possible. As more and more goods were produced, Bastiat pointed out that the tendency of that production was to drive prices down and still further down, rendering more and more material goods available to the workers and to the "common people" of society. Another truly democratic impulse stemming from modern capitalism was precisely that men had available to them the opportunity to emerge from the status of wage earners to become capitalists themselves.

The idea of savings, and the idea of individual property rights implicit in the investment of those savings, were for Bastiat the realization of the middle-class dream whereby all men in society would come to share an increasingly improved material existence. His speculations of well over a century ago have been amply demonstrated in the society of our times. Bastiat foresaw the enormous middle-class structure of present society. He foresaw the vast prosperity that could accompany a society based upon individual production and the ideal of private property. He did not foresee that we, even after such a convincing demonstration of how well freedom performs its task, would persist in political interventions that work against everything that serves as the basis for our prosperity.

Bastiat would have been quick to point out that mid-19th century France and our own era have much in common in political terms. It is true that the middle class constitutes a higher percentage of present-day American society, but the essential point is that in both societies the middle classes have assumed that placing all power in their hands would provide the solution to society's problems. The resultant "middle-class democracy" is now commonplace throughout the Western world and has repeatedly borne bitter fruit. Bastiat had already learned that lesson well between 1830 and 1848.

Economic Decisions at the Ballot Box

Bastiat also knew that economic decisions made by way of the ballot box can only have one possible outcome: an attempt to "equalize prosperity." He warned that, no matter how benevolent and generous the original intention, the underlying principle is so vicious that the end result will always be an equalization, but an equalization of poverty, not prosperity. The more schemes, the more arrangements, the more interventions in free exchange, the greater the distortions that will occur, rendering society poorer on net balance.

Viewing the blind democratic staggers of France during the first half of the 19th century, Bastiat predicted that the failure of intervention would in no way reduce the lust for further interventions:

> . . . each of us, more or less, would like to profit from the labor of others. One does not dare to proclaim this feeling publicly, one conceals it from oneself, and then what does one do? One imagines an intermediary; one addresses the state, and each class proceeds in turn to say to it: "You, who can take fairly and honorably, take from the public and share with us." Alas! The state is only too ready to follow such diabolical advice; for it is composed of cabinet ministers, of bureaucrats, of men, in short, who, like all men, carry in their hearts the desire, and always enthusiastically seize the opportunity, to see their wealth and influence grow. The state understands, then, very quickly the use it can make of the role the public entrusts to it. It will be the arbiter, the master, of all destinies. It will take a great deal; hence, a great deal will remain for itself. It will multiply the number of its agents; it will enlarge the scope of its prerogatives; it will end by acquiring overwhelming proportions.

Such a growth of political intervention is sure to reduce individual initiative. Once the intervention of the state is sufficiently massive, all initiative is stifled:

[When] we permit the makers of utopias to impose their schemes on us . . . who does not see that all the foresight and prudence that Nature has implanted in the heart of man is turned against industrial progress?

Where, at such a time, is the bond speculator who would dare set up a factory or engage in an enterprise? Yesterday it was decreed that he will be permitted to work only for a fixed number of hours. Today it is decreed that the wages of a certain type of labor will be fixed. Who can foresee tomorrow's decree, that of the day after tomorrow, or those of the days following? Once the legislator is placed at this incommensurable distance from other men and believes, in all conscience, that he can dispose of their time, their labor, and their transactions, all of which are their property, what man in the whole country has the least knowledge of the position in which the law will forcibly place him and his line of work tomorrow? And, under such conditions, who can or will undertake anything?

It is for this reason that public service nearly always eliminates competing private services. What private agency can operate effectively against a competitor completely freed from all considerations of cost? Of course, government usually takes the accompanying step of securing a perfect monopoly position by means of a law rendering its competition illegal.

The punishing price involved in the expansion of the public sector rests ultimately upon the individual citizen:

When the satisfaction of a want becomes the object of a public service, it is in large part removed from the sphere of individual freedom and responsibility. The individual is no longer free to buy what he wishes, when he wishes, to consult his means, his convenience, his situation, his tastes, his moral standards, any more than he can determine the relative order in which it seems reasonable to him to provide for his wants. Willy-nilly, he must accept from society, not the amount of service that he deems useful, as he does with private services, but the amount that the government has seen fit to prepare for him, whatever be its quantity and quality. Perhaps he does not have enough bread to satisfy his hunger, and yet the government takes from him a part of his bread, which would be indispensable to him, in order to give him instruction or public spectacles that he neither needs nor desires. He ceases to exercise free control over the satisfaction of his own wants, and, no longer having any responsibility for satisfying them, he naturally ceases to concern himself with doing so. Foresight becomes as useless to him as experience. He becomes less his own master; he has lost, to some extent, his free will; he has less initiative for self-improvement; he is less of a man. Not only does he no longer judge for himself in a given case, but he loses the habit of judging for himself. This moral torpor, which takes possession of him, likewise takes possession of his fellow citizens, and we have seen entire nations fall in this way into disastrous inertia.

Social Decisions at the Ballot Box

In his struggle to free economic decisions from the ballot box, Bastiat was faced with the charge that he lacked "social conscience":

> But, by an inference as false as it is unjust, when we oppose subsidies, we are charged with opposing the very thing that it was proposed to subsidize and of being the enemies of all kinds of activity, because we want these activities to be voluntary and to seek their proper reward in themselves. Thus, if we ask that the state not intervene, by taxation, in religious matters, we are atheists. If we ask that the state not intervene, by taxation, in education, then we hate enlightenment. If we say that the state should not give, by taxation, an artificial value to land or to some branch of industry, then we are the enemies of property and of labor. If we think that the state should not subsidize artists, we are barbarians who judge the arts useless.
>
> I protest with all my power against these inferences. Far from entertaining the absurd thought of abolishing religion, education, property, labor, and the arts when we ask the state to protect the

free development of all these types of human activity without keeping them on the payroll at one another's expense, we believe, on
the contrary, that all these vital forces of society should develop
harmoniously under the influence of liberty and that none of them
should become, as we see has happened today, a source of trouble,
abuses, tyranny, and disorder.

Our adversaries believe that an activity that is neither subsidized
nor regulated is abolished. We believe the contrary. Their faith is
in the legislator, not in mankind. Ours is in mankind, not in the
legislator.

Thus Bastiat struggled unceasingly against those who
would regulate the lives of all men. The fact that the regulation of one man by another was filtered through the intermediary of the state in no wise lessened the moral culpability involved. The basic immorality involved in coercion of men soon
corrupts not only the wielder of such power, but those over
whom the power is wielded. Soon all men come to expect that
their lives should be rendered problem-free by an omnicompe-
tent state. For this reason, Bastiat described the state as "that
great fictitious entity by which everyone seeks to live at the
expense of everyone else."

Bastiat realized that the original sin in this regard had
stemmed from the upper classes, who for so many centuries
had been willing to use political power to maintain their privileges. But he perceived almost immediately that the acquisi-
tion of political power by the middle class would only compound and not solve the problem. Soon the middle classes
were using that political power to bestow privileges upon
themselves. Not too surprisingly, the lower classes resented
the middle-class barbecue and insisted upon joining in the
privileges. The Revolution of 1848 was the result of their
insistence. In 20th-century democracy, we have eliminated the

class aspect of the problem, by moving almost all Americans into the great middle class, but we are still endeavoring to live at the expense of one another.

Education

Another fundamental conflict that Bastiat saw between the protestations and the actions of the social planners centered upon viewing men as incompetent to make their own decisions, yet presuming at the next moment that these same men were capable of deciding the course of society by means of universal suffrage. Either men are competent to make their own decisions or they are not, but the social planners must no longer be allowed to court political power by giving with one hand and taking away with the other. Bastiat saw in compulsory, publicly financed education the means by which the social architects could mold society to their will, thus being safe to advocate universal suffrage, since they were sure that the men so molded would clamor for a society centrally planned and controlled: "And why do political parties aspire to take over the direction of education? Because they know the saying of Leibnitz: 'Make me the master of education, and I will undertake to change the world.' Education by governmental power, then, is education by a political party, by a sect momentarily triumphant; it is education on behalf of one idea, of one system, to the exclusion of all others."

So long as taxes were collected by force to subsidize a public educational system, Bastiat understood that no genuine freedom of choice was present for the parent in the education of his own children. He well understood that few parents could carry the double burden of providing for the private education of their children in addition to the educational taxes, and, as the result, the state and its capacities for manipulation and indoctrination would play an ever larger role in the education of future citizens.

The Limitations of Political Solutions

Frederic Bastiat constantly returned to the theme that personal responsibility was an absolute prerequisite for dignity or freedom of any kind. Once the community has the right to decide everything and to regulate everything, the will of the individual is replaced by the will of the lawmaker and the social architect. The resultant system closely parallels the relationship between a flock of sheep and its shepherd. Government is force and force can be used legitimately only in safeguarding liberty.

Bastiat provides us with excellent advice for our own times:

> There are those who believe that a government whose authority is strictly circumscribed is the weaker on that account. It appears to them that numerous functions and numerous agencies give the state the stability of a broader base. But this is purely an illusion. If the state cannot go beyond certain definitely established limits without becoming an instrument of injustice, ruination, and plunder, without upsetting the natural distribution of industry, satisfactions, capital, and manpower, without creating potent causes of unemployment, industrial crises, and poverty, without increasing crime, without having recourse to ever more stringent repressive measures, without stirring up discontent and resentment, how will it derive any guarantee of stability from these accumulated elements of civil disorder?
>
> . . . it seems evident to me that to restrict the public police force to its one and only rightful function, but a function that is essential, unchallenged, constructive, desired and accepted by all, is the way to win its universal respect and cooperation. Once this is accomplished, I cannot see from what source could come all our

present ills of systematic obstructionism, parliamentary bickering, street insurrections, revolutions, crises, factions, wild notions, demands advanced by all men to govern under all possible forms, new systems, as dangerous as they are absurd, which teach the people to look to the government for everything. We should have an end also to ... crushing and inevitably inequitable taxation, to the ever increasing and unnatural meddling of politics in all things, and to that large-scale and wholly artificial redistribution of capital and labor which is the source of needless irritation, of constant ups and downs, of economic crises and setbacks. All these and a thousand other causes of disturbances, friction, disaffection, envy, and disorder would no longer exist; and those entrusted with the responsibility of governing would work together for, and not against, the universal harmony.

Bastiat had lived through monarchy, middle-class democracy and egalitarian democracy, each punctuated with periodical revolution. In his last days, he correctly predicted the imminent rise of dictatorship. Thus he experienced the full spectrum of political events. His genius rests on the fact that he recognized the impossibility of any lasting political solution, no matter who might control the state, so long as we fail to appreciate the necessity for individual freedom and for strict limitation of political authority to the task of protecting life and poverty.

Individual Choice and Individual Responsibility

For Bastiat, the essence of social organization rested in a single idea: "We see, then, that in almost all of the important actions of life we must respect men's free will, defer to their own good judgment, to that inner light that God has given them to use, and beyond this to let the law of responsibility take its course." He knew that human transactions were not possible in any lasting way without barter, exchange, appraisal, and value, and he knew that none of these acts of choice were possible without freedom, nor was freedom possible without responsibility. Bastiat's solution was simply stated in the phrase, "freedom of transactions":

> God has endowed mankind also with all that it needs to accomplish its destiny. There is a providential social physiology, as there is a providential individual physiology. Social organs, too, are so constituted as to develop harmoniously in the open air of liberty. Away, then, with the quacks and the planners! Away with their rings, their chains, their hooks, their pincers! Away with their artificial methods! Away with their social workshop, their phalanstery [communes], their statism, their centralization, their tariffs, their universities, their state religion, their interest-free credit or bank monopolies, their regulations, their restrictions, their moralization, and their equalization by taxation! And after vainly inflicting so many systems on the body politic, let us end where we should have begun. Let us cast out all artificial systems and give freedom a chance—freedom, which is an act of faith in God and in His handiwork.

Bastiat's Advice for Today

Frederic Bastiat had some specific advice for us concerning the means by which the admirable goal of freedom might be attained. One valuable bit of advice was his insistence upon a proper method in dealing with the social architects and all others who would undercut individual freedom. He was fond of poking fun at the pomposities of the social planner. He could use exaggeration to make a telling point. As the economist Henry Hazlitt has pointed out:

> He was the master of the *reductio ad absurdum*. Someone suggests that the proposed new railroad from Paris to Madrid should have a

break at Bordeaux. The argument is that if goods and passengers are forced to stop at that city, it will be profitable for boatmen, porters, hotelkeepers and others there. Good, says Bastiat. But then why not break it also at Angoulême, Poitiers, Tours, Orléans, and, in fact, at all intermediate points? The more breaks there are, the greater the amount paid for storage, porters, extra cartage. We could have a railroad consisting of nothing but such gaps—a negative railroad!

Another favorite tool of Bastiat's was repetition. And he also knew that points must be reduced to their simplest terms and restated in different forms so as to drive the message home. He makes clear what many modern would-be reformers forget: No amount of political activity or electioneering will establish the idea of human freedom until the idea has taken possession of the minds of men. It is in the field of education, therefore, not the field of politics, that the main battle must be fought and won.

Bastiat perceived that socialism is inevitably its own worst enemy. He argued plainly that it would destroy itself, but only after a long era of hegenomy in an increasingly statist world. He thus essentially predicted the rise and fall of socialism that we have witnessed in the 20th century.

His was the faith that "freedom works." But he did not completely regard freedom as an abstraction, any more than he considered man an abstraction as the social planners and theorists of the 19th and 20th centuries are wont to do. He knew that no amount of political tinkering or economic redistribution could cure the ills of society, but that limited government and protected private property rights could go a long way toward bringing about prosperity and equality of opportunity for individuals at all levels of society. He insisted that men were imperfect and unique, that freedom can only be

found in protecting individual life, liberty and property from
the predations of other men and *of government*. Freedom of
transaction was the particular right he hammered away at,
again and again.

Bastiat, though almost unknown today, was one of the
most important champions of freedom in the last two centuries. His life and his scholarship deserve to be re-examined in
this context, for together they represent the *whole* of the conservative tradition ranging from the economic principles of
Adam Smith to historical analysis of Alexis de Tocqueville and
the political wisdom of Edmund Burke. To these, he also adds
an even stronger emphasis than any of the others exhibit on
the compelling *moral* dimensions of free men and free markets.
For Bastiat, the essence of all economics and politics was that:

> . . . in almost all of the important actions of life we must respect
> men's free will, defer to their own good [or bad] judgment, to that
> inner light that God has given them to use, and beyond this to let
> the law of responsibility take its course.

Aphorisms

FREDERIC BASTIAT IS AMONG THE MOST QUOTABLE
of authors. It seems fitting to conclude this study of his life
with some of his aphorisms—a legacy to latter-day believers
in freedom.

Politics

I cannot legitimately force my fellow men to be industrious,
sober, thrifty, generous, learned, or pious; but I can force
them to be just.

For the same reason, the collective force cannot be legitimately employed to foster the love of labor, sobriety, thrift,
generosity, learning, religious faith; but it can be legitimately
employed to further the rule of justice, to defend every man's
rights.

* * *

Within the limits of equity, everything is to be accomplished through the free and perfectible initiative of man;
nothing is to be achieved by law or by force save universal
justice.

* * *

Try to imagine a system of labor imposed by force that is
not a violation of liberty; a transfer of wealth imposed by force

that is not a violation of property rights. If you cannot do so, then you must agree that the law cannot organize labor and industry without organizing injustice.

* * *

Unhappy country, where the sacred forces that were meant to support each man's rights are perverted to accomplish themselves the violation of these rights.

* * *

Shall I speak of the corrupting immorality that seeps into the veins of the whole body politic when, in principle, the law puts itself at the service of every spoliative impulse? Attend a meeting of the National Assembly when bonuses, subsidies, bounties, restrictions are on the agenda. See with what shameless rapacity everyone tries to make sure of his share of the plunder—plunder to which he would blush to stoop as a private individual.

* * *

The ideological war now being waged against property is neither the most bitter nor the most dangerous that it has had to contend with. Since the beginning of the world there has also been a real war of violence and conspiracy waged against it that gives no sign of abating. War, slavery, imposture, inequitable taxation, monopoly, privilege, unethical practices, colonialism, the right to employment, the right to credit, the right to education, the right to public aid, progressive taxation in direct or inverse ratio to the ability to pay—all are so many battering rams pounding against the tottering column. Could anyone assure me whether there are many men in France, even among those who consider themselves conservatives, who do not, in one form or another, lend a hand to this work of destruction?

* * *

How could men dream of blaming themselves for their woes when they have been persuaded that by nature they are inert, that the source of all action, and consequently of all responsibility, lies outside themselves, in the will of the sovereign and of the lawgiver?

* * *

Certain nations seem particularly liable to fall prey to governmental plunder. They are those in which men, lacking faith in their own dignity and capability, would feel themselves lost if they were not *governed and administered* every step of the way. Without having traveled a great deal, I have seen countries in which the people think that agriculture can make no progress unless the government supports experimental farms; that soon there will no longer be any horses, if the government does not provide studs; that fathers will not have their children educated, or will have them taught only immorality, if the government does not decide what it is proper to learn.

* * *

People are beginning to realize that the apparatus of government is costly. But what they do not know is that the burden falls *inevitably* on them.

* * *

The truth is, the word "gratuitous" as applied to public services contains the grossest, and, I may add, the most childish of fallacies. I marvel at the public's extreme gullibility in being taken in by this word. People ask us, "Are you against *gratuitous* education? *Gratuitous* stud farms?"

Quite the contrary! I'm for them and I would also be for gratuitous food and gratuitous housing. . . . if these were possible.

* * *

When a nation is burdened with taxes, nothing is more difficult, as I would say, impossible, than to levy them equally. The statisticians and fiscal authorities no longer even try to do so. What is still more difficult, however, is to shift the tax burden onto the shoulders of the rich. The state can have an abundance of money only by taking from everyone and especially from the masses.

* * *

In a country where no law may be voted and no tax may be levied save with the consent of those whom the law is to govern and upon whom the tax is to fall, the public can be robbed only if it is first deceived. Our ignorance is the *raw material* of every extortion that is practiced upon us, and we may be certain beforehand that every sophism is the precursor of an act of plunder. My friends, when you detect a sophism in a petition, get a good grip on your wallet, for you may be sure that this is what the petitioners are aiming at.

* * *

But what is most noteworthy is the astonishing blindness of the public to all this. When victorious soldiers reduced the vanquished to slavery, they were barbarous, but they were not absurd. Their object was, as ours is, to live at the expense of others, but, unlike us, they attained it. What are we to think of a people who apparently do not suspect that *reciprocal pillage* is no less pillage because it is reciprocal; that it is no less criminal because it is carried out legally and in an orderly manner; that it adds nothing to the public welfare; that, on the contrary, it diminishes it by all that this spendthrift intermediary that we call the *state* costs?

* * *

In the realm of government operation it may happen that functionaries receive services from the citizens without rendering services in return; in that case the taxpayer suffers a loss, no matter what illusion the circulation of bank notes may create.

* * *

. . . the state has no resources of its own. It has nothing, it possesses nothing that it does not take from the workers. When, then, it meddles in everything, it substitutes the deplorable and costly activity of its own agents for private activity.

* * *

. . . we must wait until we have learned by experience— perhaps cruel experience—to trust in the state a little less and in mankind a little more.

* * *

. . . the government offers to cure all the ills of mankind. It promises to restore commerce, make agriculture prosperous, expand industry, encourage arts and letters, wipe out poverty, etc., etc. All that is needed is to create some new government agencies and to pay a few more bureaucrats.

*   *   *

The state too is subject to the Malthusian law. It tends to expand in proportion to its means of existence and to live beyond its means, and these are, in the last analysis, nothing but the substance of the people.

Economics

. . . not to know political economy is to allow oneself to be dazzled by the immediate effect of a phenomenon; to know political economy is to take into account the sum total of all effects, both immediate and future.

*   *   *

Good Lord! What a lot of trouble to prove in political economy that two and two make four; and if you succeed in doing so, people cry, "It is so clear that it is boring." Then they vote as if you had never proved anything at all.

*   *   *

"In the sweat of thy face shalt thou eat bread." But everyone wants as much bread and as little sweat as possible.

*   *   *

. . . certain men have recourse to the law in order to abridge the natural prerogatives of this freedom on the part of other men. This kind of plunder is called privilege or monopoly.

*   *   *

Slavery is on its way out, thank Heaven, and our natural inclination to defend our property makes direct and outright plunder difficult. One thing, however, has remained. It is the unfortunate primitive tendency that all men have to divide their complex lot in life into two parts, shifting the pains to others and keeping the satisfactions for themselves.

* * *

Brotherhood! Sacred tie that joins soul to soul, divine spark come down from heaven into the hearts of men, how can thy name be thus taken in vain? In thy name it is proposed to stifle all freedom. In thy name it is proposed to erect a new despotism such as the world has never seen; and we may well fear that after serving as a protection for so many incompetents, as a cloak for so many ambitious schemers, as a bauble for so many who haughtily scorn human dignity, it will at last, discredited and with sullied name, lose its great and noble meaning.

* * *

This is called . . . brotherhood: "You have produced; I have not; we are comrades; let us share." "You own something; I own nothing; we are brothers; let us share."

* * *

Let a merchant begin to sell his goods on the principle of brotherly love, and I do not give him even a month before his children will be reduced to beggary.

* * *

It is indeed a singular thing that people wish to pass laws to nullify the disagreeable consequences that the law of responsibility entails. Will they never realize that they do not eliminate these consequences, but merely pass them along to other people? The result is one injustice the more and one moral lesson the less. . . .

*   *   *

The poorest class in civilized countries is far above the poorest class among savage peoples. It has risen so far; why should it not rise even higher?

*   *   *

The present level of consumption enjoyed by an honest and industrious working-class family does not surprise us because habit has familiarized us with this strange situation. If, however, we were to compare the standard of living that this family has attained with the one that would be its lot in a hypothetical social order from which competition had been excluded; if statisticians could measure with precision instruments, as with a dynamometer, its labor in relation to its satisfactions at two different periods; we should realize that freedom, despite all still-existing restrictions on it, has wrought a miracle so enduring that for that very reason we fail to be aware of it.

*   *   *

We have the distressing and unreasonable habit of attributing to *society* the suffering that we see about us. . . . To be able to assert that even the most unfortunate of men are worse off in society than out of it, we should have to begin by proving that the poorest of our fellow men has to bear, in the social state, a heavier burden of privations and suffering than would have been his lot in solitude. . . . The most impassioned advocate of the *state of nature,* Rousseau himself, admitted that . . . men did without everything . . . ; they went naked, they slept in the open air. Thus Rousseau himself, in order to present the state of nature favorably, was obliged to make happiness consist in privation. But I affirm that even this negative happiness is a delusion and that man in the state of isolation would surely die in a very few hours. Perhaps Rousseau would have gone so far as to say that that would be the true perfection. He would have been consistent, for if happiness lies in privation, then perfection lies in annihilation.

*   *   *

We are endowed with the faculty of comparing, of judging, of choosing, and of acting accordingly. This implies that we can arrive at a good or a bad judgment, make a good or a bad choice—a fact that it is never idle to remind men of when we speak to them of liberty.

*   *   *

... is it so difficult to permit men to experiment, to feel their way, to choose, to make mistakes, to correct them, to learn, to work together, to manage their own property and their own interests, to act for themselves, at their own risk and peril, on their own responsibility? Do we not see that this is what makes them men? Must we always start with the fatal premise that all those who govern are guardians and all the governed are wards?

*   *   *

For my part, it seems to me that there is a connection between the aspiration that impels all men towards the improvement of their material, intellectual and moral condition, and the faculties with which they are endowed to realize this aspiration.

Hence, I should like each man to have, on his own responsibility, the free disposition, administration, and control of his own person, his acts, his family, his transactions, his associations, his intelligence, his faculties, his labor, his capital, and his property.

*   *   *

You say that I would do better to follow a given career, to work in a given way, to use a steel plow instead of a wooden one, to sow sparsely rather than thickly, to buy from the East rather than from the West. I maintain the contrary. I have made my calculations; after all, I am more vitally concerned than you in not making a mistake in matters that will decide my own well-being, the happiness of my family, matters that concern you only as they touch your vanity or your systems. Advise me, but do not force your opinion on me. I shall decide at my *peril and risk;* that is enough, and for the law to interfere would be tyranny.

*   *   *

... since liberty is still a sacred word and still has the power to stir men's hearts, her enemies would strip her of her name and her prestige and, rechristening her *competition,* would lead her forth to sacrifice while the applauding multitudes extend their hands to receive their chains of slavery.

*   *   *

Competition is merely the absence of oppression.

*   *   *

... self-interest is that indomitable individualistic force within us that urges us on to progress and discovery, but at the same time disposes us to monopolize our discoveries. Competition is that no less indomitable humanitarian force that wrests progress, as fast as it is made, from the hands of the individual and places it at the disposal of all mankind. These two forces, which may well be deplored when considered individually, work together to create our social harmony.

* * *

Let men labor, exchange, learn, band together, act, and react upon one another, since in this way, according to the laws of Providence, there can result from their free and intelligent activity only order, harmony, progress, and all things that are good....

* * *

Shall I try to portray the state of poverty, barrenness, and ignorance in which, without the faculty of exchange, the human species would have wallowed eternally, if indeed, it would not have disappeared altogether from the face of the earth?

* * *

By virtue of exchange, one man's prosperity is beneficial to all others.

* * *

... if coercion assumes endless forms, freedom has only one. Once again, the free and voluntary transfer of services from one person to another can be defined in these simple words: "Give me this, and I will give you that. Do this for me, and I will do that for you."

* * *

In a country like the United States, where the right to property is placed above the law, where the sole function of the public police force is to safeguard this natural right, each person can in full confidence dedicate his capital and his labor to production. He does not have to fear that his plans and calculations will be upset from one instant to another by the legislature.

The Social Architects

And surely one of the saddest sights that can present itself to anyone who loves mankind is that of a productive age bending all its efforts to infect itself—by way of education—with the thoughts, the sentiments, the errors, the prejudices, and the vices of a nation of plunderers. Our age is often accused of a lack of consistency, of a failure to show any correlation between the ideals it professes and the way of life it pursues. The criticism is just, and I believe that I have here indicated the principal reason why this situation prevails.

* * *

In all things the guiding principle of these great manipulators of the human race is to put their own creation in the place of God's creation. . . .

It is true that they are optimists in regard to the future. For, although mankind, in itself incompetent, has been on the wrong track for six millennia, a prophet has come who has shown men the way to salvation; and if the flock will only be docile enough to follow the shepherd, he will lead it into the promised land where prosperity may be attained without effort, and where order, security, and harmony are the easy reward of improvidence.

* * *

All that men have to do is to permit the reformers to change, as Rousseau said, *their physical and moral constitution.*

* * *

It is the unfortunate obsession of our age to wish to give pure abstractions a life of their own, to imagine a city apart from the people who live in it, mankind independently of the individual men who constitute it, a whole aside from its component parts, collective life without the individual units that comprise it.

* * *

Though everlastingly wrangling with one another over the new institutions they would like to establish, they evince a striking unanimity in their common hatred of existing institutions, and the wage system most of all; for, if they cannot reach agreement on the social order of their choice, we must at least give them their due in that they always see eye to eye in abusing, deploring, slandering, hating, and generating hatred for anything that actually exists.

* * *

We have about a dozen reforms in progress at the same time; they press on one another like the souls of the departed before the gate to oblivion, and not one enters.

* * *

Can the human race establish a new basis for property, family, labor, and exchange every day in the year? Can it risk changing the social order every morning?

* * *

There are too many "great" men in the world; there are too many legislators, planners, founders of societies, leaders of nations, fathers of their country, etc., etc. Too many people place themselves above mankind in order to guide its footsteps; too many people make a career of being concerned with mankind.

* * *

As we have seen, the legislator, according to the ideas of the ancients, bears the same relation to mankind as the potter does to the clay. Unfortunately, when this idea prevails, nobody wants to be the clay, and everyone wants to be the potter.

* * *

But, sublime writers, kindly deign to remember sometimes that this clay, this sand, this dungheap, of which you dispose so arbitrarily, is composed of men, your equals, intelligent and free beings like you, who have received from God, like you, the power to see, to plan, to think, and to judge for themselves.

* * *

I confess that I am one of those who think that the choice, the impulse, should come from below, not from above, from the citizens, not from the legislator; and the contrary doctrine seems to me to lead to the annihilation of liberty and of human dignity.

* * *

. . . when the law, by the intervention of its necessary agent, force, imposes a system of labor, a method or a subject of education, a faith or a religion, its action on men is no longer negative, but positive. It substitutes the will of the legislator for their own will, the initiative of the legislator for their own initiative. They no longer have to take counsel together, to compare, to foresee; the law does all this for them. Intelligence becomes a useless accessory; they cease to be men; they lose their personality, their liberty, their property.

* * *

Let us, therefore, not have the presumption to overthrow everything, to regulate everything, to seek to exempt all, men and things alike, from the operation of the laws to which they are naturally subject. Let us be content to leave the world as God made it. Let us not imagine that we, poor scribblers, are anything but more or less accurate observers. Let us not make ourselves ridiculous by proposing to change humanity, as if we stood apart from it and from its errors and shortcomings.

* * *

If by ill-advised measures you free men from the responsibility of their acts, they could still be taught by theory—but no longer by experience. And I am not certain that instruction that is not reinforced and backed by experience is not more dangerous than ignorance itself.

* * *

Meanwhile, socialism has carried its folly so far as to announce the end of all the ills of society, though not of all the ills of the individual. It has not yet dared to predict that man will reach the point where suffering, old age, and death will be eliminated.

* * *

"Highway robbery," the wise men said, "is neither good nor bad in itself; that depends on circumstances. All that needs to be done is to keep things *evenly balanced* and to pay us government officials well for this labor of balancing. Perhaps pillage has been allowed too much latitude; perhaps it has not been allowed enough. Let us see, let us examine, let us balance the account of each worker. To those who do not earn enough, we shall give a little more of the road to exploit. For those who earn too much, we shall reduce the hours, days, or months during which they will be allowed to pillage."

Those who spoke in this way acquired for themselves a great reputation for moderation, prudence and wisdom. They never failed to rise to the highest offices in the state.

As for those who said: "Let us eliminate every injustice, for there is no such thing as a partial injustice; let us tolerate no *robbery,* for there is no such thing as a *half-robbery* or a *quarter-robbery,*" they were regarded as idle visionaries, tiresome dreamers who kept repeating the same thing over and over again. Besides, the people found their arguments too easy to understand. How can one believe that what is so simple can be true?

* * *

You would like to be generous and you cannot be so effectively; what I venture to ask of you is that you be just. Keep your fortune, but let me keep mine. Respect my property as I respect yours.

* * *

The admirers of unity are very numerous, and that is understandable. By a providential decree, we all have faith in our own judgment, and we believe that there is only one right opinion in the world, namely, our own. Therefore we think that the legislator could do no better than to impose it on everyone; and, the better to be on the safe side, we all want to be that legislator.

* * *

But once the legislator is elected and freed from his campaign promises, oh, then his language changes! The nation returns to passivity, to inertia, to nothingness, and the legislator takes on the character of omnipotence. His the invention, his the direction, his the impulsion, his the organization. Mankind has nothing to do but to let things be done to it; the hour of despotism has arrived.

* * *

Note that I am not contesting their right to invent social orders, to disseminate their proposals, to advise their adoption, and to experiment with them on themselves, at their own expense and risk; but I do indeed contest their right to impose them on us by law, that is, by the use of the police force and public funds.

*   *   *

For what precise and definite object are all the citizens today to be stamped, like the coinage, with the same image?

. . . On what basis would they be cast in the same mold? *And who will possess the mold?* A terrible question, which should give us pause. *Who will possess the mold?*

Man's God-Given Nature

Christianity gave to the world the great principle of the brotherhood of man. It speaks to our hearts, to our sentiments, to our noblest instincts. Political economy proclaims the same principle in the name of cold reason, and, by showing the interrelation of cause and effect, reconciles, in reassuring accord, the calculations of the most wary self-interest with the inspiration of the most sublime morality.

*   *   *

. . . even as man in his relation to his Creator is raised above the beasts by his religious feeling, in his dealings with his fellow men by his sense of justice, in his dealings with himself by his morality, so, in finding his means of survival and increase, he is distinguished from them by a remarkable phenomenon, namely, *exchange.*

*   *   *

Property is a necessary consequence of the nature of man.

In the full sense of the word, *man is born a proprietor,* because he is born with wants whose satisfaction is necessary to life, and with organs and faculties whose exercise is indispensable to the satisfaction of these wants. Faculties are only the extension of the person; and property is nothing but an extension of the faculties. . . .

There are some political theorists who are very much concerned with knowing how God ought to have made man. We, for our part, study man as God has made him. We observe that he cannot live without providing for his wants without labor, and that he will not perform any labor if he is not sure of applying the fruit of his labor to the satisfaction of his wants.

* * *

Man is cast upon this earth. He is irresistibly drawn toward happiness and repelled by suffering. Since his actions are determined by these impulses, it cannot be denied that self-interest is his great motive force as an individual, as it is of all individuals, and, consequently, of society.

From earliest childhood to extreme old age, life is a long apprenticeship. We learn to walk by repeated falls; we learn by hard and repeated experiences to avoid heat, cold, hunger, thirst, excesses. We complain that experience is a hard teacher; but if it were not, we should never learn anything.

The same is true of the moral order. The awful consequences of cruelty, injustice, terror, violence, fraud, and idleness are what teach us to be kind, just, brave, temperate, honest, and industrious. Experience takes a long time; it will, indeed, always be at work but it is effective.

Since such is man's nature, it is impossible not to recognize in responsibility the mainspring of social progress. It is the crucible of experience.

* * *

To tamper with man's freedom is not only to injure him, to degrade him; it is to change his nature, to render him, insofar as such oppression is exercised, incapable of improvement; it is to strip him of his resemblance to the Creator, to stifle within him the noble breath of life with which he was endowed at his creation.

* * *

Young men, in these times when a lamentable skepticism appears to be the effect and the punishment of our intellectual anarchy, I should deem myself happy if the reading of this book would stir you to utter those reassuring words, so sweet to the lips, which are not only a refuge from despair but a positive force, strong enough, we are told, to remove mountains, those words that begin the Christian's profession of faith: *I believe.*

The Future

Every attempt to divert responsibility from its natural course is an attack upon justice, freedom, order, civilization, or progress.

* * *

Where are we going? The Assembly must direct itself by some principle; it must commit itself to justice everywhere and for everybody, if it is not, in fact, to rush headlong into the system of legal and reciprocal plunder, to the point of completely equalizing all classes, that is, to the point of communism.

* * *

... gentlemen, organize industry as much as you please. But we, for our part, will take care to see that you do not organize *robbery*.

* * *

It is not, as people think, the monopolists, but the monopolized, that sustain the monopolies.

* * *

When misguided public opinion honors what is despicable and despises what is honorable, punishes virtue and rewards vice, encourages what is harmful and discourages what is useful, applauds falsehood and smothers truth under indifference or insult, a nation turns its back on progress and can be restored only by the terrible lessons of catastrophe.

* * *

When education has sown a fatal seed in the soil of public opinion, there is in the body politic a force of self-preservation, *vis medicatrix,* that enables it to rid itself, at long last, after many sufferings and tears, of the baneful germ with which it has become infected.

* * *

... it takes time for enlightenment to be produced and propagated, and that, insofar as enlightenment is achieved, right no longer needs to be maintained by might, and society regains possession of itself.

* * *

What is freedom? It is the sum total of all our freedoms. To be free, on one's own responsibility, to think and to act, to speak and to write, to labor and to exchange, to teach and to learn—this alone is to be free.

* * *

It can further be affirmed that, thanks to the nonintervention of the state in private affairs, wants and satisfactions would develop in their natural order. We should not see poor families seeking instruction in literature before they have bread. We should not see the city being populated at the expense of the country, or the country at the expense of the city. We should not see those great displacements of capital, of labor, and of population that are provoked by legislative measures, displacements that render the very sources of existence so uncertain and precarious, and thereby add so greatly to the responsibilities of the government.

* * *

I have not made an alliance with anyone; I have not joined either side. On each question, I have voted according to my own conscience.

Index

179